WINNER
GOURMAND
World Cookbook Awards

THE BEST OF

EPICURE'S

VEGETARIAN CUISINES

OF THE WORLD

ASHA KHATAU

For my husband, Mahendra Khatau,

who is the main inspiration behind

this book and my quest for excellence.

ISBN 81-7693-084-9

BPI (INDIA) PVT LTD

© Asha Khatau

Reprint 2005

BPI (INDIA) PVT LTD
3, Tara Bhavan, F-344/1, Old M.B. Road,
Lado Sarai, New Delhi-110 030
Tel.: 51665005/06, Fax : 51665736
e-mail: bpipl@vsnl.com

Branch : 24/26, Champa House, Krantiveer Rajguru Marg
Girgaon, Mumbai 400 004
Tel.: 23872677, 3873940
e-mail: bpipl@bpiindia.com

While the publisher has taken all reasonable care in the preparation of this book the publisher make no representation, express or implied, with regard to the accuracy of the information contained in this book and cannot accept any legal responsibility or liability for any errors or omission from the book or the consequences thereof.

Cover Design : **Neve /** Neetu Mishra

e-mail: nevedesigns@vsnl.net

Cover Copyright © BPI (INDIA) PVT LTD

FOREWORD

The vegetarian gourmet is always at pains to discover new recipes, new cuisines, new tastes and flavours. It is in an effort to provide a greater choice to those who are vegetarian and yet savour the best of the world's cuisines, that I present this book.

There is the fettucine, gnocchi and pepperonata from Italy, quesadillas, tostadas and guacamole from Mexico, fondue and röesti from Switzerland and exotic delights from South East Asia, like Thai curry and raw papaya salad. Then there are the wonders of Chinese lettuce wrap, Mongolian barbecue, Japanese miso soup and tempura, as well as Lebanese delicacies like falafel, hummus and baklava. Also included are sections which cover the various cuisines of Europe.

The recipes have been divided according to the cuisines to which they belong. I have created a separate section for drinks and desserts from around the world. The objective is to provide simple yet interesting and authentic menus to the enterprising cook. It may come as a surprise that Indian recipes are not included in this particular collection. The omission is intentional as vegetarian Indian cuisine forms the content of Volume II.

Following the overwhelming response to my *Epicure* cooking classes, I offer this book to the lovers of vegetarian food, keeping in mind the need for meals that are both satisfying and simple to make. There is an old saying, 'good cooking begins in the market', therefore I request all my readers to plan their meals after finding out about the availability of the ingredients and then choosing the recipes. A meal engages all the senses – taste, smell, touch, sight and sound. All these elements work together to capture the attention of those eating. A perfect meal will draw people together with dishes that are delicious, while they enjoy one another's company. Through this book I would like to pass on some of my own joys and discoveries which I hope will in turn inspire you towards perfection. Through this you will develop the 'quality of caring' – the secret ingredient in your food.

ACKNOWLEDGEMENTS

To the One above, for making me so strong and capable.

The putting together of *Epicure's Vegetarian Cuisines Of the World* happened with the constant support, encouragement and help of many people whom I wish to thank. Firstly my heartfelt thanks to my immediate family – my husband Mahendra Khatau, my three children – Priya, Shreya and Manish. My mother-in-law Mrs. Leela Khatau, and my mother Mrs. Sudha Sampat, both of whom have been my pillars of strength every step of the way. My sister-in-law Ameeta Thackersey and my sister Hina Bhatia, have been involved in encouraging, giving new ideas, trying out my experiments and supporting me in every way. Typing out recipes on the computer and editing them became a lot easier with their help. My special thanks to my brother-in-law, Jagdish Thackersey, for taking wonderful cover photos.

I would also like to thank all those who helped me during my photoshoot for this book. Leena Thackersey, Neomy, Heena Zaveri, Sunanda, Jyoti Seth, Niti Desai and Vidya Saxena. During this time I have to mention my hard working staff Vinod, Mahadev, Santosh, Naresh and Gopinath. They worked day and night with me.

This book would not have existed without two people from BPI – Jai Saxena and Chandralekha Maitra. I am grateful to both of them.

Last of all, my close friends and my cooking class students cannot be forgotten in my vote of thanks, as they are the ones eagerly waiting for my work to emerge. I thank them deeply for giving me inspiration to write the recipes, cook them, perfect them and put them together in a book. I wish them, and my readers, luck and happiness with their cooking.

Contents

The influence of Chinese food on Indians has been tremendous over a long period of time. This has been mainly due to their hot and spicy, sweet and sour combinations, which are very close to Indian tastes. Their variety of vegetables, staple grain, rice and noodles, give vegetarians a wide range of sumptuous dishes which all add a zing to their lives.

Authentic ingredients are easily available now, due to their constant demand and increasing popularity. The recipes specify authentic Chinese ingredients, so that you can savour the flavour of original Chinese food, brought by immigrant Chinese people to our country. Chinese tea is a must from the beginning to the end of a Chinese meal. It helps to digest the spicy food and neutralize its effect.

CHINESE
CUISINE

VEGETABLE MANCHOW SOUP

ingredients

6 cups	Clear vegetable stock
	(½ cup cabbage, 3 carrots, 5-6 celery stalks, 1 spring onion with leaves, 4 florets cauliflower, washed, chopped and cooked in 8 cups of water for 20 minutes. Use just the water without liquidising.)
2 tbsp(each)	Finely chopped tomato, capsicum, green onions, cabbage, carrot and cauliflower
1 tbsp(each)	Finely chopped coriander, mint, garlic, and ginger
3 tsp	Soy sauce
2 tbsp	Corn flour mixed with 1 cup water
½ tsp	MSG (optional)
2 tbsp	Oil

To Garnish
Chilli oil and crispy noodles

To Serve
Green chillies in vinegar

method

Heat the oil in a wok or saucepan on a high flame. Add mint, coriander, garlic, ginger and the chopped vegetables along with the MSG (if using) and fry for 3-4 minutes. Add the stock, soy sauce and salt. When the soup begins to boil, add the corn flour mixture and boil further for one minute, top with chilli oil and crispy noodles. Serve piping hot with chillies in vinegar.

Opposite (clockwise)
i) Manchow Soup ii) Crispy Seaweed
iii) Red Garlic Sauce iv) Soy Chilli Sauce

LETTUCE WRAP

ingredients

10-12	Iceberg lettuce leaves
2 cups	Finely chopped vegetables (French beans, carrots, bean sprouts, cabbage, spring onions, etc.)
2 tbsp	Coarsely powdered peanuts
2 tbsp	Sesame oil
1 tbsp	Finely chopped garlic
1 tbsp	Soy sauce
1 tbsp	Red chilli paste
1 cup	Plum sauce (recipe follows)
	A pinch of MSG (optional)

* You will need a hot plate to serve

Wash and rinse the whole lettuce leaves in cold water. Drain and set aside in a cool place. In a medium sized frying pan, heat the oil. Fry the garlic briefly, add the vegetables and stir fry on a high flame, add MSG (if using) and cook for 4-5 minutes. Add soy sauce, chilli paste and salt to taste. Take it off the gas and add the peanuts. Do not over cook the vegetables. Set aside until used.

PLUM SAUCE

Mix together 1 clove of garlic, minced with ½ tsp salt, 1 tsp dried basil, ¼ tsp thyme, 2 tbsp vinegar, 1 tsp parsley, ½ cup plum jam and 2 tbsp soy sauce. Mix until all the ingredients are well blended and place in a serving bowl.

How to Serve

On a glass plate, put all the lettuce leaves upside down. Leave the vegetables on the hot plate and the sauce in a bowl. Take one lettuce leaf, spread 1-2 tsp of the plum sauce all over it and place 2 tsp of the vegetable mixture in the centre. Wrap up the leaf into a roll and serve immediately. This is usually assembled at the table.

Opposite (clockwise from top)
i) Shanghai Vegetable Stir Fry   ii) Red Garlic Sauce
iii) Hunan Fried Rice   iv) Pan Fried Hakka Noodles

SESAME VEGETABLE FRITTERS

ingredients

6	Large carrots cut into 3" long pieces
2	Large capsicums cut into 3" long pieces
6	Large florets cauliflower
6	Baby corn
6	Broccoli
4 tsp	Baking powder
1 tbsp	Soya sauce
1 tbsp	Vinegar
½ tsp	Chilli powder
½ tsp	Pepper
1 tsp	Sugar
¼ tsp	MSG (optional)
3 tbsp	Sesame seeds
	Salt to taste

For the Batter

½ cup	Plain flour
½ cup	Corn flour
1 tsp	Ground ginger
1 ½ cups	Water
1 tsp	Lemon juice
	Salt to taste
	Oil for frying

To Serve
Chilli sauce

method

Prepare a mixture of all the ingredients except the vegetables. Marinate the sliced vegetables in this sauce for half an hour. Stir and shake two to three times. Drain off the excess liquid. Prepare a smooth batter with water. Dip each piece in the batter and deep fry in oil till light brown in colour. Serve with Chilli Sauce.

Serves 6-8

Steamed Wantons

ingredients

16	Wonton wrappers
10 cups	Water
¼ cup	Finely chopped French beans
½ cup	Finely chopped green onions
¼ cup	Finely chopped carrots
½ cup	Finely chopped cabbage
¼ tsp (each)	Ginger and garlic, crushed
½ tsp (each)	Sugar and pepper
1 tsp	Soy sauce
3 tbsp	Oil
4 tbsp	Finely chopped green onions and garlic for tempering
	Salt to taste
	A pinch of MSG (optional)

To Serve
Green Chilli Sauce (recipe follows)

method

In a frying pan, heat 1 tbsp oil on a high flame, add all the vegetables, ginger, garlic and MSG (if using). Fry for 1 minute. Add sugar, salt, pepper and soy sauce. Take it off the gas. Let it cool. Place a single wonton wrapper on the cutting board, put 1 tbsp of the filling on it and gather the edges together in the desired shape and seal it with a mixture of corn flour and water (paste). While you are doing this, set water to boil and add 1 tbsp salt and drop 6-8 wontons into the boiling water at a time. Cook uncovered for 10 minutes. Watch the wontons floating to the surface. Drain, and remove. In a large frying pan heat 2 tbsp of oil and fry the green onions and garlic briefly. Add well-drained wontons to this and stir only by shaking the pan and not using a spoon or else the wontons will break. Serve at once with Green Chilli Sauce.

Green Chilli Sauce

To make ½ a cup of the sauce, mix together 1 tbsp each of finely chopped coriander, green chillies, garlic and powdered sugar. Add 3 tbsp of lemon juice or white vinegar along with ½ cup of water. Add salt to taste.

Stays fresh for 1-2 days only.

Serves- 4

Chilli Garlic Potatoes

ingredients

250 gms	Small potatoes boiled and skinned
1	Green chilli chopped
3-4	Dry red chillies ⎫ make into paste
1 clove	Garlic ⎭ with water
2 tbsp	Soy sauce
1 tbsp	Vinegar
2 tbsp	Tomato ketchup
1+1 tbsp	Oil
½ tsp	MSG (optional)
	Salt and pepper to taste

method

Prick the potatoes with a fork. Mix together soy sauce, vinegar, tomato ketchup, 1 tbsp oil, salt and pepper. Soak potatoes in this mixture for 2-3 hours. Heat 1 tbsp of oil in a frying pan, fry chilli-garlic paste with ¼ cup of water and cook for 1 minute. Add soaked potatoes and MSG (if using). Cook till the sauces dry out. Serve hot with toothpicks as a starter or just as an accompaniment to your Chinese meal.

CRISPY SEAWEED

ingredients

750 gms	Seaweed or Green cabbage leaves
1 tsp	Salt
1½ tbsp	Castor sugar
	Oil for frying

To Garnish
2 tsp toasted sesame seeds or fried split almonds

method

Wash and dry the seaweed or cabbage leaves and shred them with a knife into the thinnest possible shavings. Dry them out thoroughly. Heat oil in a deep fryer. Before it gets too hot, turn off the heat for ½ a minute, add the cabbage shavings and turn the heat on again to medium high. Stir and when they start to float to the surface, scoop them out gently with a slotted spoon and drain on paper towels. Sprinkle the salt and sugar evenly on top. Garnish with sesame or almonds and serve.

Serves 4

RED GARLIC SAUCE

ingredients

1 tbsp	Finely chopped garlic
1 tsp	Finely chopped green chillies
2 tbsp	Finely chopped green onions
1 tbsp	Finely chopped onions
2 tbsp	Oil
1 tbsp	Red chilli paste
2 tbsp	Tomato purée
1 tsp	Sugar
1 tsp	Soy sauce
½ tsp	Vinegar
	A pinch of MSG (optional)

method

Heat the oil in a small saucepan. Fry the garlic, green chillies, green onions, and onions. Sauté for 3-5 minutes. When soft, add red chilli paste, tomato purée, soy sauce, MSG (if using), sugar, vinegar and salt. Cook further for two minutes and let it cool to room temperature.

Makes 1 cup

MONGOLIAN BARBECUE

ingredients

Vegetables

250 gms	Cabbage, shredded
250 gms	Carrots, shredded
250 gms	Red, yellow and green capsicum, cut long
250 gms	Yellow corn kernels, boiled
200 gms	Baby corn, cut long
1 bunch	Green onions, cut with leaves
200 gms	Onions, cut into thin slices and halved
250 gms (1 pkt)	Bean sprouts, washed and dried
250 gms	Asparagus, cut into 3 inch long pieces
200 gms	Snow peas, washed (if available)
200 gms	Bean curd, shredded
250 gms	Water chestnuts, skinned and cut into quarters
4	Eggs, hard boiled and cut into slices (optional)
250 gms (1 pkt)	Mushrooms, washed with hot water and sliced lengthwise

Seasonings

* You will need 4 identical bowls for the seasonings.

¼ cup	Finely chopped ginger
¼ cup	Finely chopped garlic
¼ cup	Sesame seeds, toasted
¼ cup	Peanuts, coarsely chopped and toasted

Sauces and Water
* You will need 8 identical bowls for the sauces and waters.

Sugar Water
½ cup sugar dissolved in ¼ cup of water

Ginger Water
½ cup water mixed with 3 tbsp of chopped ginger and ½ tsp salt

Garlic Water
½ cup water mixed with 3 tbsp finely hopped garlic and ½ tsp salt

Soy Sauce ¼ cup dark sauce mixed with ¼ cup water

Chilli Vinegar In ¼ cup white or brown vinegar mix ¼ cup water, ½ tsp salt, 1 tsp sugar and 5-6 finely chopped green chillies.

Chilli Oil
Heat ½ cup of sesame oil, take it off the gas and immediately put 3tbsp of chilli powder and ½ tsp of salt. Cool it.

Sweet and Sour Sauce
Mix together, in a saucepan, ¼ cup tomato sauce, 3 tbsp vinegar, 2 tbsp sugar, ¼ cup water, 1 tbsp corn flour, salt and pepper to taste. Place it on the fire and heat slowly. When it boils, simmer for 2 minutes. Remove from heat and cool.

Chilli Garlic Sauce
Soak 8 dry red chillies in water for 30 minutes. Mix together 10 cloves of garlic, 2 tbsp vinegar, 2 tbsp sugar, 1 tbsp oil, salt to taste and 1 tsp soy sauce. Put this mixture in a grinder and make it into a smooth paste. Add extra water for required consistency.

how to proceed

You will need a big Chinese wok or a large barbecue plate ready on the fire. Now each individual takes a soup plate or a largish bowl. Pick up all the vegetables of your liking and add all the sauces and seasonings to your taste. Now stir-fry this on a high flame for 3-4 minutes. Serve this with steamed rice, fried rice or noodles as per your choice. The rice or noodles can be mixed with the vegetable mixture while stir-frying. Each individual should make their own mixture to their choice.

STEAMED RICE

ingredients

1 cup	Long grained rice
2 cups	Water
1 tsp	Salt
1 tbsp	Oil

method

Wash and soak the rice for 20 minutes. Boil the water, add the salt and oil. Add the rice and cook until tender for approximately 20 minutes. Remove from heat and allow it to cool. Separate the grains with a fork.

EGG FRIED RICE

ingredients

2	Eggs, lightly beaten
¼ cup	Finely chopped green onions
2 tbsp	Oil
1 cup	Long grained rice
	A pinch of MSG (optional)

method

Cook the rice as explained for steamed rice. Heat oil in a wok, fry the onions for 1 minute, add MSG (if using) and eggs. With a wooden spatula work the eggs into thin shreds. When slightly set, add rice and salt to taste. Serve hot.

NOODLES

100 gms	Uncooked noodles
1 tsp	Oil
2 tsp	Salt
8 cups	Water

method

Boil the water. Add the salt and oil. Add noodles and cook uncovered for 7-8 minutes. Drain well and cool thoroughly.

Shanghai Vegetable Stir Fry

ingredients

250 gms	Fresh mushrooms, cut lengthwise
150 gms	Broccoli, cut into 1 inch pieces
150 gms	Fresh asparagus, cut into 1 inch pieces
1 cup	Bean sprouts
½ cup	Chopped cashews or almonds
5 tbsp	Oil
1 tsp	Sugar
1 tbsp	Soy sauce
1 tsp	Corn flour mixed with 1 tbsp of cold water
100 gms	Bean curd, cut into cubes
2 cloves	Chopped garlic
2 tbsp	Finely chopped capsicum

method

Heat oil in a casserole dish or a saucepan. Fry bean curd until golden, remove and put aside. In the same pan add garlic, capsicum and cashew and fry briefly, add all the vegetables and continue frying on a high flame for 3-4 minutes. Add salt, sugar and soy sauce, simmer for 5-7 minutes. Increase the heat to high, add corn flour mixture and cook uncovered for 2 minutes.

Serve hot.

HUNAN MEIN CHOW
Hunan Fried Rice

ingredients

2½ cups or 500 gms	Long grained rice (wash and soak for ½ an hour)
1 bunch	Finely chopped spring onions
½ cup	Finely chopped capsicum
½ cup	Green peas, boiled
½ cup	Corn kernels, boiled
½ cup	Finely chopped French beans
¼ cup	Almonds, cut into small pieces
¼ cup	Walnuts, shelled and cut into small pieces
1 tbsp	Ginger-garlic paste
½ tsp	Pepper powder
¼ tsp	MSG (optional)
2 tbsp	Soy sauce
½ cup	Oil
	Salt to taste

method

Boil the rice with ½ tsp salt and ½ tsp oil over a medium flame, stirring occasionally, until tender but not over cooked. It's very important to ensure that every grain of rice is separate. Drain and set aside. In the remaining oil, fry the nuts, remove and set aside. In the same oil over a high flame, stir fry the French beans, carrots and capsicum for 2 minutes. Add spring onions, ginger-garlic paste and finally the green peas and corn, along with the MSG (if using) and cook for 5 minutes over a high flame. Add soy sauce, salt and pepper. Add cooked and cooled rice. Quickly stir-fry it. Adjust the salt. Turn it out on a serving plate and garnish with fried nuts. Serve hot.

Serves 6-8

Mixed Vegetables
Sichuan Style

ingredients

100 gms	Cauliflower, cut into 1 inch pieces
100 gms	Baby corn, cut into 1 inch pieces
100 gms	Chinese cabbage, cut into square pieces
100 gms	Green beans, cut into 1 inch pieces
100 gms	Carrots, cut into 1 inch pieces
3-4 stems	Spring onions
1" piece	Ginger, finely chopped
2 cloves	Garlic
2 tbsp	Soy sauce
1 tbsp	Chilli bean paste (¼ cup Soya beans + 10 red chillies)
1 tsp	Sugar
2 tsp	Corn flour mixed with ¼ cup water
1 tbsp	Vinegar
1 tsp	Sichuan peppercorn
2 tbsp	Sesame oil

method

Heat oil in a wok on a high flame. Add spring onions, ginger, garlic and chilli paste. Fry for one minute. Add the rest of the vegetables and continue cooking till the vegetables are soft. Now add soy sauce, sugar and vinegar. Finally add corn flour mixture. Cook for 1 more minute and serve immediately. Serve with Sichuan Sauce (recipe follows).

SICHUAN SAUCE

Grind together 20 soaked red chillies with 5 cloves of garlic to a smooth paste. Heat 3 tbsp of oil in a frying pan. Add 1 tbsp chopped garlic, 1 tsp chopped green chilli, 1 tsp grated ginger, 2 tbsp chopped onions and fry for 1 minute. Add the paste and fry again. Add 1 tbsp vinegar with ½ cup vegetable stock. Mix well. Add 2 tsp sugar, 2 tsp lemon juice, salt, MSG (optional), and 1 tbsp corn flour mixed with 2 tbsp of water. Cook for 1 minute stirring constantly. Serve hot.

Makes 1 ½ cups

Pan Fried Hakka Noodles

ingredients

1 pkt(200 gms)	Hakka Noodles
1 + 2 tbsp	Oil
100 gms	Carrots, shredded
100 gms	French beans, chopped long
1 cup	Cabbage, shredded
1	Small capsicum, shredded
100 gms	Bean sprouts
2	Spring onions, chopped
2 tbsp	Butter
1 tsp	Sugar
1 tbsp	Vinegar
1 tbsp	Soy sauce
3-4	Red chillies, broken into pieces
2 tsp	Chopped garlic
8 cups	Water for boiling
	A pinch of MSG (optional)
	Salt and pepper to taste
	A little butter for sizzling

method

Boil 8 cups of water in a vessel. Add the noodles and cook for 3-4 minutes. Drain and rinse under cold water and toss with 1 tbsp of oil to prevent them from sticking to one another. Set aside. Heat 2 tbsp of oil in a wok on a high flame. Add all the vegetables, the MSG (if using), red chillies, garlic and fry for 3-4 minutes. Add the cooked noodles, butter and all the other spices. Cook until the sauces dry up. Serve on a hot sizzler plate. Pour butter around the noodles. Serve immediately.

Vegetarianism in Thailand is partly due to the prevailing Buddhist influence and partly due to economic reasons. Any kitchen in which Thai food is being cooked, becomes a beehive of activity i.e. sautéing, grilling, frying, pounding, grinding, juicing and chopping. Thai cuisine has an extensive variety of raw material from dry spices to noodles and rice to vegetables to key ingredients like lemon grass, basil and kaffir lime leaves. The expert composition of all these unique flavors will give the vegetarian enthusiast a delicious Thai meal. To be able to obtain the authentic Thai taste, these ingredients have to be correct as they play an important part in Thai cooking. The basic rule for Thai cooking is that all the ingredients should be ready before the cooking begins. The actual cooking takes only a few minutes. Come, enjoy the pleasure of cooking a vegetarian Thai meal with tried and tested recipes, which are sure to leave a long lasting impression on your tastebuds.

Thai Cuisine

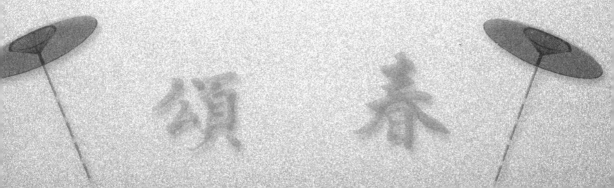

HOT AND SOUR VEGETABLE SOUP
Tom Yam Chai

Ingredients

For the Soup

3 cups	Vegetable stock (recipe follows)
1 tsp	Chopped lemon grass
3	Kaffir Lime leaves
2 tbsp	Soy sauce
2 tbsp	Lime juice
1 tbsp	Spicy chilli oil (recipe follows)
¾ cup	Mushrooms, quartered
¼ cup	Tofu, cut into square pieces
¼ cup	French beans, cut long

To Garnish

Coriander leaves

For the Vegetable Stock

1	Medium sized onion, chopped
2	Carrots, chopped
2	Celery stalks, roughly chopped
4	Coriander roots , chopped
1 tsp	Black peppercorns
5 cups	Water

For the Spicy Chilli Oil

½ cup	Tamarind pulp
1 cup	Thinly sliced shallots
¼ cup	Oil
$\frac{1}{3}$ cup	Chopped garlic
10	Chopped dried red chillies
5	Chopped fresh green chillies
½ cup	Water
½ cup	Sugar
5 tbsp	Soy sauce

method

For the Soup

In a large pan, bring the vegetable stock to a boiling point, and stir in all the ingredients except the chilli oil to this mixture. Simmer and stir well until the vegetables are cooked. Add spicy chilli oil, garnish, and serve immediately.

Serves 4

For the Vegetable Stock

Boil the water in a large pan. Add the onions, carrots, celery, coriander roots, and the peppercorns to the water and boil until the quantity has reduced to half. Cool, liquidise, strain and set aside.

Makes 3 cups

For the Spicy Chilli oil

Heat oil in a pan over medium heat. Add garlic, shallots and chillies. Sauté until tender. Turn off the heat and put all the ingredients into a grinder along with the water and grind to a fine paste. Pour the paste back into the oil and add the tamarind pulp, sugar and soy sauce. Reduce over medium heat for 20 minutes until the surface becomes glossy. Do not over cook.

Makes approximately 1 cup

Thai Coconut Cream Soup
Tom Ka Phad

ingredients

2 tbsp	Sesame or corn oil
1 tbsp	Red or green Thai curry paste
200 gms	Tofu, cut into ½" strips
100 gms	Green beans, cut into ½" wide strips
2 small	Eggplants, cut into 1" pieces
100 gms	Broccoli florets
3 cups	Vegetable stock
3 cups	Coconut milk mixed with 1 tbsp corn flour
1 tbsp	Light soy sauce
¼ cup	Fresh basil, chopped
2-3	Red or green chillies, slit
3-4	Kaffir lime leaves
2-3 sticks	Lemon grass
	Salt and pepper to taste

method

Heat the oil in a large saucepan over medium heat. Add the curry paste and fry briefly. Add the vegetables and cook for 3-5 minutes until they are well coated with the paste. Add broth, coconut milk, and soy sauce and bring to a boil. Make sure all the vegetables are soft. Add the tofu, basil, kaffir lime leaves, lemon grass, salt and pepper. Garnish with slit chillies and serve hot.

Serves 4-6

Raw Papaya Salad
Som Tham Mara Gor

ingredients

3 cups	Green Papaya, peeled deseeded and grated
5 cloves	Garlic
3	Small red chillies
½ cup	Green beans, cut into 1½ inches in length
3 tbsp	Lemon juice
3 tbsp	Peanuts, roasted and crushed
1 tbsp	Light soy sauce
1 tbsp	Palm sugar
2 tbsp	Tamarind juice
1 tsp	Salt
1	Medium sized tomato, chopped
2	Large leaves of Chinese cabbage OR one head iceberg lettuce

method

In a mortar, lightly pound garlic and chillies. Turn this out in a large bowl, add papaya and mix thoroughly. Add the peanuts, tomato, green beans, salt, lemon juice, soy sauce, tamarind juice and palm sugar. Mix thoroughly and chill. Arrange the Chinese cabbage or lettuce on a serving dish and turn the salad into it. This tastes especially good with sticky (glutinous) rice.

SWEET CORN CAKES
Tod Man Khao Pohd

ingredients

2½ cups	Raw sweet corn off the cob (roughly chopped)
1 tbsp	Curry powder
2 tbsp	Rice flour
3 tbsp	Wheat flour
½ tsp	Salt
2 tbsp	Soy sauce
	Oil for deep frying

To Serve
Honey Chilli Sauce (recipe follows)

method

In a bowl, mix all the ingredients together, except the oil. Mix well, make a thick dough. Heat the oil. Using a spoon, form the dough into small cakes and slide them into the hot oil. Deep fry them until golden brown. Drain the excess oil and allow them to cool slightly. Serve with Honey Chilli Sauce.

Serves 6-8

HONEY CHILLI SAUCE

ingredients

2 tbsp	Honey
½ tsp	Salt
1	Finely chopped small red chilli
4 tbsp	Vinegar OR Lemon juice
1 tsp	Corn flour
¼ cup	Water

method

Mix all the ingredients in a small saucepan and give it one boil. Cool thoroughly.

Makes approximately ¹/₃ cup

Pattaya Baby Corn

ingredients

200 gms	Baby corn
1 tbsp	Light soy sauce
¼ cup	Vegetable oil
1 tbsp	Sugar
2 tbsp	Shredded kaffir lime leaves

For the Spice Mixture

3	Dried red chillies
3	Cloves garlic
1 tsp	Grated galangal
½ tsp	Coriander seeds
½ tsp	Chopped coriander root
1 tbsp	Thinly sliced shallots
2 tbsp	Finely chopped lemon grass
½ tsp	Grated lemon rind
1 tsp	Salt

method

Grind together all the ingredients for the spice mixture in a mortar until well ground. Drop baby corn into boiling water, boil for 3 minutes and drain. In a wok or frying pan, heat oil. Fry the spice mixture until dried and fragrant and season with sugar and soy sauce. Now add baby corn and work it around to thoroughly mix with the spices. Sprinkle a little water if it feels too dry or sticks to the pan. Turn it out on a serving plate and sprinkle sliced lime leaf. Serve with toothpicks.

MIXED VEGETABLE SATAY
Satay Ped Pak

ingredients

For the Marinade

1 tsp	Finely chopped galangal or ginger
1 tsp	Finely chopped lemon grass
2	Coriander roots
4 cloves	Coarsely chopped garlic
½ tsp	Ground black pepper
2 tbsp	Curry powder
1 tbsp	Soy sauce
2 tbsp	Sugar
1 tsp	Coriander seeds
1 tsp	Ground cumin
1 tsp	Salt
2 tbsp	Oil
½ cup	Thick coconut milk
2 cups	Mushrooms
3	Capsicums, cut into cubes
6-8	Babycorn, cut into 2" pieces
100 gms	Cauliflower, cut into small florets
6-8	Baby onions

For the Peanut Sauce

1 tbsp	Oil
1 tbsp	Red curry paste
1 cup	Thick coconut milk
2 tbsp	Sugar
½ tsp	Salt
1 tbsp	Lemon juice
3 tbsp	Roasted and ground peanuts

method

For the Marinade

In a grinder pound together the ginger, lemon grass, lime leaf, coriander root and garlic to form a paste. Place this in a mixing bowl and stir in all the other ingredients including all the vegetables. Leave for 30 minutes. After that, take a piece of each vegetable and thread it onto a satay stick. Apply a little oil on a tray and place the satay sticks on it. Grill until the vegetables are cooked thoroughly. Serve with Peanut Sauce.

PEANUT SAUCE

In a saucepan, heat the oil, add the curry paste and fry briefly until it blends with the oil. Add the coconut milk, lower the heat and stir well until a rich red colour appears. Add the remaining ingredients, stirring constantly until a thick sauce is formed. Set aside to cool.

Makes approximately 1 cup

SPICED CHILLI DIP
Nam Prik

ingredients

2	Fresh large green chillies
4	Small red chillies
2 large cloves	Garlic, peeled
4	Small shallots, peeled
1	Medium sized tomato
1	Round green aubergine
2 tbsp	Lemon juice
2 tbsp	Soy sauce
½ tsp	Salt
1 tsp	Sugar

To Serve
A selection of fresh vegetables such as asparagus, baby corn, red, yellow and green peppers and spring onion

method

Wrap the first 6 ingredients in foil and place under a hot grill until they begin to soften. Remove from the heat and place in a blender. Pound together to form to soft liquid paste. Add the remaining ingredients to the paste in turn, stirring well. Turn into a bowl and serve with your selection of fresh vegetables.

Serves 6-8

Stir Fried Vegetables
Phad Phak

ingredients

2 tbsp	Oil
1 tsp	Garlic, finely chopped
3	Large dried red chillies, coarsely sliced
½ cup	Roasted cashew nuts
100 gms	Green beans, chopped into 1 inch lengths
100 gms	Baby corn, cut into 1 inch lengths
6 pieces	Spring onions, cut lengthwise
3 tbsp	Vegetable stock
1½ tbsp	Soy sauce
½ tsp	Sugar
1 cup	Bean sprouts

To Garnish
Coriander leaves
Carved vegetables such as carrots and turnip

method

In a wok, heat oil. Fry garlic until golden brown. Add all the other ingredients in turn, stirring constantly on a high flame. Turn onto a serving dish and garnish with coriander leaves and carved vegetables.

GOLD BAGS
Tung Tong

ingredients

10-12	Wonton/Spring roll wrappers
1 tbsp	Chopped garlic
1 tbsp	Coriander roots
1 tsp	Whole black peppercorns
1½ cups	Boiled and mashed potato
1 cup	Finely diced water chestnuts
2 tbsp	Roasted ground peanuts
1 tbsp	Soy sauce
½ tsp	Salt
½ tsp	Sugar
1 tbsp	Corn flour mixed with hot water
	Oil for deep frying

To Serve
Hot and Sweet Sauce

method

For the Gold Bags

In a mortar, pound the garlic, coriander root and peppercorns to form a paste. In a bowl, mix the paste with all the other ingredients and stir thoroughly. Place 1½ tbsp of this mixture on each wrapper. Bring the opposite sides of the triangle to form another triangle. Then, gather in the other two corners to form a pouch. Put a little corn flour in the gathers of the pouch to hold it together. Fluff out the gathers to make it look like a money bag. Deep fry until golden brown. Drain and serve with the Hot and Sweet Sauce.

For the Hot and Sweet Sauce

Heat together 6 tbsp vinegar with 4 tbsp sugar and ½ tsp salt until the sugar dissolves, allow it to cool and pour into a serving bowl. Stir in chopped red and green chillies (1 each)

Opposite (clockwise)
i) Gold Bags   ii) Corncakes with Honey
Chilli Sauce   iii) Raw Papaya Salad

CURRY PASTE RICE

ingredients

1 cup	Thai Jasmine rice or long grained rice
2-3 tbsp	Red Thai curry paste
3-4 tbsp	Sesame oil
3-4	Kaffir lime leaves
3-4	Basil leaves
	Salt and sugar to taste

To Garnish
2-3 stems spring onions and a bunch of basil leaves

method

Wash and soak rice for ½ an hour. Boil 2 cups of water in a medium sized pot, add soaked rice and cook briskly. Remove from heat just before it is completely cooked (approx. 7-8 minutes). In another medium sized pan, heat oil and fry curry paste briefly. Add cooked rice, Kaffir lime leaves, basil, salt and sugar. Mix well until rice is thoroughly coated with the paste. Turn it out on a serving plate, garnish with spring onions and basil and serve hot.

Opposite (clockwise)
i) Steamed Rice ii) Red Thai Curry
iii) Spiced Chilli Dip

MIXED VEGETABLE GREEN CURRY
Gaeng Pedpak Wan

ingredients

For the Curry

2-3 tbsp	Green curry paste (recipe follows)
2 cups	Thin coconut milk
½ cup	Thick coconut milk mixed with 1 tbsp cornflour
½ cup	Vegetable stock
100 gms	Small eggplant
1 cup	Chopped fresh mushrooms
½ cup	Bean curd, sliced long
½ cup	Shelled and boiled green peas
½ cup	Cauliflower, cut into small florets
¼ cup	Bamboo shoots (optional)
1 tsp	Salt
1 tbsp	Sugar
3	Kaffir lime leaves
3	Small fresh green chillies
15	Basil leaves
2 tbsp	Oil

method

For the Curry

Heat the oil. Add the curry paste, fry briefly and stir. Then add the egg plant, mushroom and green chillies and stir well. Add salt and let the vegetables cook. When they are nice and soft, add the rest of the vegetables. Mix well. Add the rest of the ingredients ending with the basil leaves. Stir constantly. Serve hot.

*Remember – do not over boil or else the coconut milk will curdle. Serve with steamed rice.

Note Adjust the quantity of paste as per your requirement of spices.

Serves 4-6

GREEN CURRY PASTE

ingredients

For the Green Curry Paste

1 tbsp	Chopped ginger or galangal
1 tsp	Grated lemon rind or chopped kaffir lime leaves
½ tsp	Cumin seeds
1 tsp	Coriander seeds
1 tsp	Black peppercorn
10	Small green chillies
3 tbsp	Chopped fresh coriander
2 tbsp	Coarsely chopped shallots
1 tbsp	Chopped lemon grass
2 tbsp	Coarsely chopped garlic
½ tsp	Salt
1 tbsp	Finely chopped coriander root

method

Place fresh coriander in a grinder with 1 tbsp cold water, grind to a paste. Put it through the strainer, discard pulp and reserve the juice and put it back into the blender. Add ginger, lemon rind, powdered spices, lemon grass garlic, shallots, salt, chillies and coriander roots. Grind to a fine, smooth paste.

MIXED VEGETABLE RED CURRY
Gaeng Ped Pak

ingredients

2 tbsp	Oil
2 tbsp	Red curry paste (recipe follows)
1 cup	Thin coconut milk
½ cup	Thick coconut milk mixed with 1 tbsp corn flour
½ cup	Sweet corn kernels
½ cup	Long beans, cut into 1 inch pieces
½ cup	Spring onion, cut lengthwise into 1 inch pieces
½ cup	Carrots, cut into 1 inch pieces
½ cup	Bean curd, cut into small cubes
1 tbsp	Light soy sauce
1 tsp	Salt
1 tsp	Sugar
3	Kaffir lime leaves
2	Fresh red chillies, cut lengthwise
15	Thai basil leaves

method

Heat the oil in a large saucepan and briefly fry the paste. Add all the vegetables with thin coconut milk. Stir well. Add rest of the ingredients except the coconut cream, and stir the mixture well. Let the vegetables cook to your liking. Now add thick coconut milk. Just before serving arrange fresh red chillies and basil leaves on top and serve immediately with rice.

Serves 4-6

RED CURRY PASTE

ingredients

2 tbsp	Finely chopped galangal or ginger
¼ cup	Finely chopped lemon grass
1 tbsp	Kaffir lime leaves or grated lemon peel
2 tbsp	Finely chopped garlic
¼ cup	Finely chopped shallots
7	Red chillies, dried (spicy variety)
7	Kashmiri red chillies, dried
1 tsp	Salt
1 tbsp	Coriander seeds
¼ - ½ cup	Water to make paste

method

In a frying pan dry roast the coriander seeds and chillies for 2-3 minutes. Remove from heat and place them in the grinder, add all the other ingredients to form a thick paste. Store in a jar until used. Can be kept in the refrigerator for two weeks and in the freezer for two months.

Note   a)   Do not over boil the curry or else it may curdle.

        b)   To make 1 cup thin coconut milk, mix ½ grated coconut with 1 cup water, liquidise and strain.

        c)   To make ½ cup thick coconut milk, mix ½ grated coconut with ½ cup water, liquidise and strain.

Makes 1 cup

VEGETARIAN THAI NOODLES
Pad Thai

ingredients

200 gms	Dry Sen Lek noodles (soaked in water for 30 minutes and drained)
1 cup	Bean-curd, cut into ½ inch cubes
½ cup	Turnip, cut long
4	Spring onions, cut into 1 inch pieces
4 tbsp	Roasted and chopped peanuts
1 ½ cups	Bean sprouts
2 cloves	Garlic
1 tsp	Chilli powder
4 tbsp	Soy sauce
2 tsp	Sugar
2 tbsp	Lemon juice

To Garnish
1 sprig of coriander
1 lemon wedge

For Optional Egg Variation

2	Eggs
1 tbsp	Finely chopped fresh coriander
2	Finely chopped green chillies
½ tsp	Salt

method

In a wok, heat the oil until a light haze appears. Add bean curd and stir briefly. Add noodles, stir well then add the turnip, spring onions, ½ the peanuts, and ½ the bean-sprouts. Stir well, then add the chilli powder, sugar, soy sauce and lemon juice. Stir well and turn onto a plate. Sprinkle with remaining peanuts and chopped coriander. Arrange the remaining bean-sprouts (to be mixed in at the table just before serving), and put lemon wedge on the side of the plate.

Egg Variation

After the noodles are ready, set them aside. In a large non-stick frying pan heat 1 tsp oil and in a bowl on the side, break eggs and beat them until light and fluffy. Add coriander, chillies and salt. Turn this mixture into the heated frying pan. Cover with the same sized plate or a frying-pan cover and let it cook on medium heat for 45 minutes. Place hot noodles onto a serving plate, cover with the omelette and garnish. Serve immediately.

GOLDEN BASKETS

ingredients

10-12	Ready baskets or tart cases
2 tbsp	Oil
1 tsp	Chopped garlic
$\frac{2}{3}$ cup OR	
100 gm	Sweet corn kernels, boiled
1	Large onion, finely chopped
1	Large potato, finely chopped and boiled
1 tbsp	Soy sauce
½ tsp	Salt
1 tsp	Curry powder
½ tsp	Turmeric powder
½ tsp	Pepper
2	Small red chillies, finely chopped

To Garnish
Coriander leaves, finely chopped

method

In a frying pan, heat oil and fry the garlic and chillies. Stir constantly. Add all the spices and vegetables in turn and mix well. When the mixture is well coated remove from heat and allow it to cool slightly. Then fill the baskets with the mixture. Garnish each with a few coriander leaves and serve.

The Japanese eat first with their eyes. Their formal meal consists of a series of exquisite dishes that are as beautiful as they are delicious. Japanese people are known for the greatest longevity amongst all the people of the world. This is mainly due to their well-balanced food. From seafood to soya beans and high fibre vegetables to valuable carbohydrate products, there is little room for fat in their diet. Though it is very difficult to find vegetarian Japanese food, I have made an effort to come up with a menu that can give you the satisfaction of authentic Japanese food, not to forget the slimming Japanese green tea which is a must before, during and after the meal.

Japanese
Cuisine

頌

新年

謹賀新年

おめでとう

春

INTRODUCTION TO TEMPURA

To be successful in tempura frying the batter should be right. It should be mixed just when the oil is ready. The batter should be as cold as possible to give a light, crispy, non-greasy finish. If the quantity of tempura is more, make the batter in two batches. For frying, sesame oil gives a deep rich aroma. While frying, the surface of oil should not be more than 60% of the surface area. This is essential for each piece to be fried properly.

TEMPURA VEGETABLES WITH DIPPING SAUCE

ingredients

For the Tempura

2 cups	Plain flour
¼ tsp	Baking soda
⅛ tsp	Salt
1 tbsp	Rice flour OR
1	Egg yolk, beaten
13 fl oz	Ice water
500 gms	Vegetables (such as zucchini, asparagus, mushrooms, carrots, broccoli, egg plant, bell peppers), cut into strips
	Peanut oil for frying
	A pinch of MSG (optional)

For Sauce 1

2 cups	Vegetable Stock	
2 tbsp	Sake	
½ cup	Soy sauce	Boil and cool
2 tbsp	Grated radish	
1 tbsp	Grated ginger	

Opposite (clockwise)
i) Tempura Vegetables with Raddish-Ginger-Soy Dipping ii) Miso Soup   iii) Japanese Cucumber Salad

For Sauce 2

3 tbsp	Soy sauce
2 tbsp	Sherry
1 tbsp	Spring onion, finely chopped
1 tsp	Sugar
1 tsp	Sesame seeds
	A few splashes of chilli sauce

method

For the Sauce

Combine all the ingredients and set aside.

For the Tempura

In a medium sized mixing bowl stir together plain flour, soda, salt and MSG (if using). Make a well in the centre, add the yolk or rice flour and ice water at once and stir till combined.

In a deep frying pan heat oil. Dip the dry vegetables into the batter, a few pieces at a time, swirling to coat. Fry in hot oil for 2 minutes till golden. Remove from the oil. Drain on a rack with a paper towel and serve immediately with both the sauces.

Opposite (clockwise)
i) Ramen Noodles with Vegetables ii) Takikomo Rice
iii) Sesame Sauce iv) Teppanyaki Vegetables

Miso Soup

ingredients

2	Onions, diced
⅔ cup	Minced carrot
2	Large Chinese cabbage leaves, minced
4 tsp	Oil
3 tbsp	Miso Paste
8 cups	Thin stock
2 tsp	Tahina paste

To Garnish

½ cup	Bean curd, cubed
2	Spring onions, chopped
1 tsp	Dry mustard powder

method

Heat oil in a sauce pan, sauté the onion, carrot and cabbage for 5 minutes. Add miso, water, tahina paste and bring to a boil. Simmer for 20 minutes. Garnish, simmer for 1 minute and serve.

Serves 4

JAPANESE CUCUMBER SALAD
Kyuri No Sunome

ingredients

5	Medium sized cucumbers, cut lengthwise with skins
2 tsp	Salt
½ cup	Lemon juice
½ cup	Sugar
¼ tsp	MSG (optional)
1 tbsp	Wine vinegar
2 tsp	Toasted sesame seeds

method

In a large bowl, slice the cucumbers, apply salt, mix well with your hands and set aside for 45 minutes. Meanwhile, mix lemon juice, sugar, MSG (if using) and wine vinegar. Set aside. Transfer cucumbers to a strainer and squeeze as much liquid as possible out of the cucumber. Discard the salt water, add the lemon juice mixture to the cucumber and sprinkle sesame seeds over it and refrigerate till ready to use.

POTATO CROQUETTES

ingredients

2 tbsp	Oil
1 tbsp	Minced ginger
¼ cup	Chopped spring onion
2 cups	Boiled and mashed potato
1 cup	Green peas, boiled and crushed
¼ cup	Carrots, boiled and chopped into small pieces
2 tbsp	Soy sauce
2 tbsp	Cornflour
1 tbsp	Vinegar
1 tbsp	Sugar
3 tbsp	Plain flour
	Salt and pepper to taste
	Breadcrumbs

method

Heat the oil. Add the ginger and spring onions, stir for half a minute. Add potatoes, peas, carrots, soy sauce, cornflour, black pepper, vinegar, salt, sugar and pepper. Mix well. Remove from heat and cool. Shape them into a cylindrical form of approximately 2" length and then roll in the crumbs and deep fry in oil. Serve with Sesame Sauce (recipe follows).

Serves 8-10

Sesame Sauce

ingredients

3 oz	Sesame seeds, toasted
¼ cup	Japanese soy sauce
¼ cup	Sesame oil
1 tbsp	Vinegar
4 tbsp	Water
1 clove	Garlic, crushed
1½ tsp	Red pepper or Togarashi
1 tsp	Chopped white onion

method

Grind some sesame seeds in a small blender. Add soy sauce, oil, vinegar, water, onion, red pepper and garlic. Blend well until combined. Serve this sauce at dinner in individual small dishes.

TEPPANYAKI VEGETABLES

ingredients

| 1 kg | Vegetables such as asparagus, mushrooms, snow peas, babycorn, bean sprouts, carrots, peppers etc., cut into 1" inch pieces and washed |
| | Oil for stir frying |

For the Seasoning Sauce

3 tbsp	Sake or wine vinegar
2 tbsp	Water
1 tbsp	Finely chopped garlic
½ tsp	Chopped ginger

method

Heat the teppanyaki plate or large frying pan. Pour a little oil, add freshly cut vegetables and fry for 2-3 minutes. Mix together all the ingredients for the sauce and dribble over the vegetables. Cook for 2-3 minutes more and serve on a hot plate.

Serves 4-6

TAKIKOMO RICE

ingredients

500 gms	Thick variety rice, rinsed, soaked and drained
500 ml	Water
1 tbsp each	Sake and soy sauce
300 gms	Vegetables such as peas, yellow corn, onions, carrots
100 gms	Bean curd, lightly fried in oil
1 tsp each	Sugar, salt and pepper
3 tbsp	Soy sauce
2 tbsp	Sake
2 tbsp	Sesame oil
3	Eggs, beaten (optional)

Seasoning Sauce

method

Cook the rice in 500 ml. water with sake and soy sauce, so that each grain is separate, drain and set aside. On a teppanyaki plate or in a wok, place the seasoning sauce and stir-fry the vegetables till tender. Add rice and tofu and mix well. Serve in individual bowls. (If using egg, add the beaten eggs just before adding rice).

RAMEN NOODLES WITH VEGETABLES
Moyashi Soba

ingredients

For the Noodles

250 gms	Ramen noodles
3 cups	Vegetable soup stock *(Roughly chop 1 onion, 2 carrots, a head of Pak Choy, a few leaves of Chinese cabbage and 1 tomato. Boil vigorously in 8 cups of water with a bayleaf. Simmer for 1 hour and strain stock)*

For the Topping

1	Leek, cut into 2" long strips
10-12	Snow peas, cut into half
½ cup	Bean sprouts
½ cup	Sliced button mushrooms
1	Courgette, cut into 2" strips
100 gms	Tofu, cut into cubes and fried
2-3 cloves	Garlic, sliced

To Fry and Season

1 tbsp	Soy sauce
1 tbsp	Sesame oil
½ cup	Water or stock
½ tsp	Corn flour mixed with 2 tbsp water
	Salt and pepper to taste

To Garnish

1	Spring onion

method

Wash and prepare vegetables for stir-frying. Heat the oil, add all the vegetables and stir-fry for 2 minutes. Then, add ½ cup water or stock and season with soy sauce, salt and pepper. Finally, thicken with corn flour mixture. Boil the noodles to required consistency and place them in a serving bowl. Pour the boiling stock over them and arrange the stir-fried vegetables on top. Garnish with spring onion and serve immediately.

Serves 4-6

The territory south of the United States presents a whole new world of cookery. The warm climate of Mexico influences eating habits in the country. The foods are festive, colourful, healthy and easy to make and they certainly do present an attractive complement to entertainments. The tortilla, a flat pancake of maize or wheat flour, is the bread of the people. It can be used in the form of a taco, a tostada, an enchilada or a quesadilla. Beans form the staple food. And, enviably, there are chilli peppers in degrees of hotness and sweetness, which defy definition. Soups, rice and vegetable stews are other important items of daily fare. Sidewalk cafés lure passers-by to stop for coffee, a cup of chocolate or a sip of tequila. Whatever the meal, whatever the season, every meal in Mexico is served with music and colour.

The increasing popularity of this cuisine has prompted many stores to carry a complete line of Mexican ingredients. All these provide great scope for interesting vegetarian fare.

Mexican Cuisine

TORTILLA SOUP

ingredients

500 gms	Tomatoes (blanched)
1	Small onion (quartered)
1 clove	Garlic
500 ml	Vegetable stock (2 cups water + 2 stock cubes)
½ tsp	Chilli powder
½ tsp	Salt
¼ tsp	Pepper
¼ tsp	Ground coriander
¼ tsp	Cumin
1 tbsp	Fresh coriander (freshly cut)
2-3	Jalapeño peppers, finely chopped
¼ cup	Cooking oil
6	Corn tortillas 6" in diameter (made with ½ cup maize flour, 1 tbsp plain flour and salt)

To Serve
Sour Cream, Tortilla Chips and Monterey Jack Cheese (shredded)

method

Place the tomatoes, onions and garlic in a blender or food processor, blend till smooth. Transfer to a large saucepan. Add the stock, seasonings Jalapeño peppers and coriander, bring to a boil. Reduce heat and simmer for 3 minutes. Cut tortillas into ¼ wide and 3" long strips. Fry in hot oil until crisp and brown (to make it low-cal, bake it in the oven with a little sprinkling of oil). Ladle the soup into bowls. Top with tortilla chips, sour cream and cheese.

Serves 4

CHEESE QUESADILLAS

ingredients

8	Corn tortillas
½ cup	Monterey Jack cheese
½ cup	Cheddar cheese
½ cup	Maize flour
½ cup	Plain flour
¾ cup	Water
3-4	Jalapeño peppers, finely chopped
2-3 tbsp	Olive oil
1	Finely chopped onion
1 tsp	Taso seasoning mix

method

To make corn tortillas mix the maize flour with enough warm water to make the dough hold together well. Shape the dough into 8 parts. Roll it with light even strokes to form 4-5 inch diameter rounds and turn onto a preheated ungreased griddle over a medium heat. Cook both sides till lightly flecked with brown specks. Keep warm.

For the Quesadillas
Making quesadillas is like making a tortilla sandwich. Mix both the cheeses, Jalapeño peppers, onion and taco seasoning, spread this mixture evenly on a tortilla, top with the other tortillas, press it to seal all the sides. Put oil on the skillet, fry them on medium heat, cook for 2 minutes. Turn over and brown the other side. Remove and cut each into quarters. Serve hot with Red Salsa.

TORTILLA ROLL-UPS

ingredients

3	10" tortillas
150 gms	Cream cheese
2 tbsp	Finely chopped red and green peppers
1	Finely chopped spring onion
2 tbsp	Finely chopped Jalapeño pepper
1 tbsp	Finely chopped parsley
1 tbsp	Taco seasoning
1 clove	Garlic, minced (optional)

To Garnish
2-3 sprigs parsley

method

In a bowl mix all the ingredients excepts the tortillas, using a wooden spoon. Place one tortilla on a chopping board, spread $\frac{1}{3}$ of the mixture evenly, then roll it tightly. Proceed for the remaining tortillas in the same way. Wrap these rolls in a piece of foil and chill. When you want to serve, remove the foil and slice each one at an angle (approximately 2" in length) and arrange on a plate decorated with 2-3 sprigs of parsley. Serve chilled.

Serves 6-8

CHILI CON QUESO

ingredients

450 gms	Monterey Jack cheese and Sharp Cheddar or Nacho cheese
2	Jalapeño peppers, finely chopped
2 stems	Spring onions
2 cloves	Garlic
200 gms	Red tomatoes, blanched
½ tsp	Salt
1 tsp	Taco seasoning mix
½ tsp	Worcestershire sauce
	A pinch of dried oregano
1 tbsp	Plain flour

To Serve
Corn chips or crackers

method

Cut the cheese, and onions into chunks. Combine all the ingredients in a food processor and blend till finely chopped. Pour into a chafing dish or fondue pot. Heat till the cheese melts. Serve hot with corn chips or crackers.

Mexican Corn Tartlets

ingredients

For the Tartlets

½ cup	Maize flour
¼ cup	Plain flour
1 tsp	Salt
1 tbsp	Oil

For the Filling

1 cup	Yellow American corn, boiled
2	Jalapeño peppers, chopped
2	Medium sized tomatoes, chopped
1	Onion, finely chopped
2-3 cloves	Garlic, chopped
3 tbsp	Red or Green peppers, finely chopped
2 tbsp	Olive oil
3 tbsp	Grated cheese
1 tsp	Salt
1 tsp	Paprika

method

For the Tartlets

Make a soft dough with both flours, salt and oil. Divide the dough into 4 parts. Take one part, roll it out into a 7" round and cut 4 smaller rounds out of it, that you will be able to fit into small tart cases. Repeat this with all the 4 rounds. Prick with a fork and lightly bake in a hot oven at 350°F for 10-15 minutes, until crisp. Remove from the oven and let them cool. Makes 12-15 tart cases. Store in air-tight container.

For the Filling

Heat oil in a medium frying pan. Add garlic and onion and fry for 2-3 minutes. Add peppers and jalapeño. Cook until soft. Add tomatoes and cook for a minute more. Then add the corn, salt and paprika. Mix well. Just before serving add cheese. Fill the mixture in the tartlets while the mixture is hot and serve immediately with salsa.

Serves 6-8

Mini Fajitas With Pico De Gallo

ingredients

500 gms	Mixed vegetables, cut into 1" strips (peppers, green onions, carrots, beans, mushrooms)
1 tsp	Vegetable stock powder
1 tsp	Taco seasoning
2	Medium sized onions, cut into rings and halved
½ cup	Olive oil
12	Corn tortillas (4" rounds)

method

Marinate the vegetables in olive oil and stock powder for at least 1 hour. Put half the marinating oil in a thick pan, sauté onion and add the marinated vegetables with the juice and taco seasoning. Cook until the vegetables are soft. Turn it out onto a heated plate and serve with warm tortillas and Pico de Gallo (recipe follows).

PICO DE GALLO

ingredients

4	Jalapeño peppers, chopped
2 stems	Green onions, chopped
5	Medium sized tomatoes, chopped
2 tbsp	Chopped coriander leaves
2 tbsp	Oil
1 tbsp	Vinegar
1 tsp	Taco seasoning
	Salt to taste
	A pinch of oregano

method

Combine all the ingredients and chill.

Makes 1 cup

Potato Skins With Cheese And Salsa

ingredients

4	Medium sized potatoes
2 tbsp	Olive oil
2 tbsp	Monterey Jack cheese, grated
2 tbsp	Mozzarella cheese, grated

For the Salsa

1 cup	Firm, ripe tomatoes, diced and deseeded
2 tbsp	Thinly sliced spring onions
1 tbsp	Finely chopped green pepper
1 tbsp	Finely chopped coriander
½ cup	Corn kernels, boiled
1 tsp	Finely chopped jalapeño pepper
1 tsp	Taco seasoning
2 tsp	Olive oil
1 tbsp	Minced garlic
1 tbsp	Lemon juice

To Serve
Salsa and Sour cream

method

Pre heat the oven to 400°F. Wash the potatoes thoroughly, pierce with the tip of a knife and bake directly on the oven rack until tender, for about 45 minutes. Let the potatoes cool. Meanwhile make salsa. In a bowl, combine all the ingredients and mix well. Set aside. Halve the potatoes lengthwise and using a teaspoon, carefully remove all but $\frac{1}{8}$ th inch of the potato leaving the skin intact. Reserve the inside of the potato for some other use. Brush the inside of the potato shell lightly with olive oil. Place potato skins on a baking sheet and bake for 5 minutes. Turn the skins over and bake on the other side for 5 minutes. Spoon the salsa over potato skins, dividing evenly. Sprinkle with both the cheeses and bake till cheese melts. Serve immediately with extra salsa or sour cream.

Serves 4-6

Aloha Loaf

ingredients

2 cups	Finely grated cheese
¼ cup	Thick cream, beaten
½ tsp	Lemon juice
¼ cup	Minced green pepper
2 tbsp	Minced parsley
1 cup	Tomatoes, blanched, deseeded and chopped
1 cup	Finely chopped red pepper
2 tbsp	Powdered peanuts
100 gms	Cream cheese
1 tbsp	Finely chopped garlic
	A dash of Tabasco
	Salt and pepper to taste

To Garnish
Parsley sprigs, pineapple, kiwi slices, thinly sliced ginger

To Serve
Crackers or Melba toast

method

Line a 9"x5" loaf pan with waxed paper and set aside. In a small bowl combine the Cheddar cheese, cream, lemon juice, green pepper, Tabasco, salt and pepper. Spread this mixture on the bottom of the loaf pan. Sprinkle minced parsley, and lightly press on to the top of the cheese layer. Refrigerate this mixture for 2 hours. In another bowl combine the tomato, red pepper, peanut powder, cream cheese, garlic, salt and pepper. Spread this over the chilled cheese mixture. Refrigerate for 2 more hours. When the loaf is frozen invert the loaf onto a serving dish, remove the paper, garnish with ginger, parsley sprigs, kiwi and pineapple slices. Serve with crackers and melba toast.

Serves 8-10

Red Salsa

ingredients

4	Tomatoes, cut into large pieces
1	Onion, cut into large pieces
5-6	Cloves of garlic
4	Dry red chillies, soaked in water
1 tbsp	Vinegar
1 tbsp	Chopped coriander leaves
2 tbsp	Chopped Jalapeño peppers
1 tsp	Taco seasoning
	A large pinch of oregano
	Salt to taste

method

To make Salsa sauce put all the ingredients into a food processor but take care not to pureé it. When you want chunky salsa, simply chop all the vegetables finely and mix them in a bowl.

Makes 1 cup

Refried Beans

ingredients

200 gms	Rajma, dark (kidney beans)
2-3	Cloves of garlic
1	Onion, roughly chopped
2 tbsp	Taco seasoning
2 tbsp	Red salsa
	Salt to taste

method

Soak Rajma overnight for 6-8 hours. To cook them, put them in a pressure cooker with onions, garlic and salt. Cook until soft. Remove from the pressure cooker and mash lightly, add taco seasoning and salsa. Use this mixture as taco or burrito filling or as an accompaniment to mexican meal.

Makes 3 cups

GUACAMOLE

ingredients

1	Ripe avocado
2-3 tbsp	Lemon juice
1 tbsp	Fresh, chopped coriander
2-3	Chopped green chillies or jalapeño peppers
2 cloves	Garlic, minced
2-3 tbsp	minced onion
1	Tomato, peeled, deseeded and chopped
1 tbsp	Mayonnaise
	Salt to taste

method

Peel, cut and mash the avocado with a fork while blending in the lemon juice. Add salt, coriander, chillies, garlic, onion, tomato and mayonnaise. Mix thoroughly and chill. Serve chilled with tortilla chips.

Makes 1 cup

SOUR CREAM

ingredients

1 cup	Thick Yogurt
100 gms	Fresh Cream
2 tbsp	Lemon juice OR White Vinegar
½ tsp	Salt
1 tbsp (each)	Minced garlic, finely chopped chives

method

Chill yogurt and cream separtely. Beat the cream and fold it in the yogurt, now add lemon juice, salt, garlic and chives. Chill thoroughly and use as an accompaniment to your mexican meal.

Opposite (clockwise)
i) Margarita ii) Corn and Bean Burritos iii) Nacho Chips with Red Salsa, Refried Beans, Guacomole, Sour Cream and Grated Cheese

GUACAMOLE MOULD

ingredients

1 envelope	Gelatine
¼ cup	Cold Water
1 cup	Vegetable stock (1 cup water and 1 stock cube)
2	Large ripe avocados, cut into cubes
2 tbsp	Lemon juice
½ cup	Thick yogurt
2 tsp	Grated onion
2 tbsp	Chopped jalapeño peppers
½ tsp	Taco seasoning
2 cloves	Garlic, crushed
	Salt to taste
	A dash of Tabasco

To Serve
Tortilla chips

method

In a small pan mix the gelatine and cold water. Let it stand for 3-4 minutes. In the meanwhile, heat the stock in another pan and pour it over the gelatine mixture and boil again until dissolved. Set aside. In a liquidiser jar, place avocados, lemon juice, onion, jalapeño peppers, salt, taco seasoning, Tabasco and garlic. Start the motor and liquidise all the ingredients. While the motor is running, slowly pour in the gelatine mixture in a thin stream until evenly distributed. Transfer the mixture to a large bowl and fold in the yogurt. Pour into a 4 cup oiled mould. Refrigerate for 4-6 hours until firm. To serve, unmould by dipping in hot water and then invert onto a plate. Decorate with parsley, olives etc. Serve with tortilla chips.

Opposite (clockwise)
i) Tortilla Soup ii) Mexican Vegetable Rice

Seven Layered Mexican Dip With Nacho Chips

ingredients

200 gms	Rajma (kidney beans)
3 tbsp	Vinegar
500 gms	Onions
4 tsp	Taco Seasoning
500 gms	Tomatoes
2 tbsp	Coriander
100 gms	Garlic
½ tsp	Mustard
2 cups	Yogurt
1 tsp	Chilli powder
50 gms	Red chillies
1 tbsp	Mayonnaise
½ cup	Olives
1 tbsp	Cream cheese
½ cup	Jalapeño peppers
	Salt to taste
½ cup	Spring onions
2-3	Green chillies
1	Avocado
100 gms	Fresh cream
250 gms	Monterey Jack or Cheddar cheese

the layers

i) Rajma Soaked overnight, boiled in a pressure cooker with one chopped onion, 2-3 cloves of garlic and a pinch of salt

ii) Sour Cream 2 cups of yogurt tied in a cloth and then sieved with 200 gms of cream

iii) Avocado   1 medium sized avocado (ripe), mashed with a fork and seasoned with lemon

iv) Olives Half a cup of sliced ripe greens olives

v) Cheese One cup of grated cheese

vi) Salsa   4 tomatoes, cut into large pieces
1 onion, cut into large pieces
5-6 cloves garlic
1 tbsp vinegar
1 tbsp chopped coriander
1 tsp taco seasoning
4 red Kashmiri chillies
2 tbsp chopped Jalapeño peppers
Salt to taste

vii) Jalapeño peppers   ½ cup, sliced

viii) Spring onions   finely chopped

method

i) Mash the beans with 1 tsp of taco seasoning and 2 tbsp salsa and set aside.

ii) Place the sieved yogurt in a bowl, add lightly beaten fresh cream, 1 tsp vinegar, salt and a pinch of oregano. Chill.

iii) To the avocado, add ½ tsp mustard, 2 chopped green chillies, 1 tbsp mayonnaise, 1 tbsp cream cheese, ½ tsp chopped garlic, 1 grated onion and one chopped tomato. Set aside to chill in the refrigerator.

iv) To make the salsa, put all the ingredients into a food processor but take care not to purée it, too much.

how to proceed

In a flat pie dish spread the bean mixture evenly, layer the salsa on top, followed by the peppers, olives, spring onions and grated cheese. At this point, bake it in the hot oven for 7-8 minutes. Remove from the oven and spread the avocado mixture and sour cream right on top and serve immediately with nacho chips.

Makes one 8" round pie dish

LAYERED RICE SALAD WITH SALSA

ingredients

For the Rice

2 cups	Long grained rice
5½ cups	Water
1½ tsp	Salt
1 tbsp + 1 tsp	Olive oil

For the Red Salsa

2-3	Jalapeño peppers
3-4 cloves	Garlic
1 tbsp	Coriander
½ tsp	Salt
1 tbsp	Vinegar
1 tsp	Taco seasoning
	A pinch of oregano
2 cups	Tomatoes, chopped
1	Onion, chopped

} Blend together to make a sauce

1 cup	Finely chopped red pepper
½ cup	Finely chopped onion
1 tbsp	Olive oil

For the Green Layer

1 ½ cups	Chopped green peppers
¾ cups	Chopped onion
½ cup	Chopped fresh basil
2 tbsp	Olive oil

For Sour Cream Layer

1 cup	Thick yogurt
1 tbsp	Lemon juice
½ cup	Fresh cream
2 cloves	Garlic, crushed

To Garnish
Sliced Jalapeño peppers, Basil leaves and Sour cream

method

For the Rice
Combine the water, olive oil and salt in a large saucepan. Bring to a boil, add rice and boil again. Reduce heat to low. Cover and cook until the liquid has been absorbed and the rice is tender yet firm. Fluff up the rice with a fork. Transfer to a baking sheet and cool completely. Season to taste with salt and pepper. Divide this rice into two parts, one for the green and one for the red.

For the Green Layer
In a small frying pan heat 2 tbsp of olive oil. Briefly fry the green peppers and onions until they are semi soft. Add the basil, take it off the gas, mix this with one half of the rice and set aside.

For the Red Layer
Prepare the salsa in a food processor, remove into a bowl, add red pepper, onion and olive oil and toss the other half of the rice in it.

For the Sour Cream Layer
Mix all the ingredients together and keep chilled.

to assemble the salad

In a transparent glass bowl, spread the green layer evenly at the bottom. Then, spread the red layer over it and finally cover the top with the sour cream and garnish with jalapeños or basil leaves. Chill the salad for 1-4 hours and serve.

CORN TOSTADOS

ingredients

For the Tostados

1 ¼ cups	Maize flour
¾ cup	Plain flour
½ tsp	Oregano
3 tbsp	Oil
	Salt to taste
	Oil for deep frying

For the Topping

2 tbsp	Butter
4-5	Green chillies (chopped)
1	Capsicum (chopped)
2 tbsp	Plain flour
¾ cup	Milk
¼ cup	Cheese
250 gms	Fresh corn kernels (boiled) or tinned
	Salt to taste

To Garnish

Shredded cabbage and chopped onions

method

For the Tostados

Make dough out of flour, maize flour, salt, oregano, oil and water. Knead well and divide into 20 portions. Roll each portion to a thin round of 4 inches diameter. Deep fry in oil till light brown in colour. While still hot, press in the base of a metal cup to get a depression in the centre of the tostados. Store in an airtight box.

For the Topping

Heat the butter and sauté green chillies and capsicum till soft. Add flour and milk. Stir till thick like a sauce. Now mix in the corn, cheese and salt to taste. Simmer till the mixture is thick. Spread the hot corn topping on each tostado. Pour 2 tsp of salsa and cheese on it. Bake it in the oven till the cheese melts. Garnish with shredded cabbage and chopped onions and then serve immediately.

CORN AND COTTAGE CHEESE BAKED IN GRILLED TOMATO SAUCE

ingredients

2 cups	Yellow corn kernels, boiled
1 cup	Cottage cheese, cubed
½ cup each	Onions and red or green peppers, cut into cubes
2+1 tbsp	Butter
2+1 tbsp	Olive oil
1 tsp each	Salt and taco seasoning
1 tsp	Garlic, chopped
½ tsp	Dried oregano
1 tbsp	Finely chopped jalapeño peppers
1 recipe	Tomato sauce (recipe follows)

To Garnish
1 cup Sour cream with chives

method

In a saucepan heat butter and oil together. Fry garlic, oregano and jalapeño peppers for 1 minute. Add the onions and peppers and fry again until the vegetables are soft. In a small frying pan, toss the cottage cheese cubes with 1 tbsp of oil for about 1 minute until slightly brown. Now add the corn and cottage cheese to the pepper mixture. Season with salt and taco seasoning and set aside.

For the Tomato Sauce
To make the grilled tomato sauce take 1 kg of medium sized tomatoes, grill them over coal or over a rack with skewers. Grill until the skins blister and char slightly. Pull off the skins and roughly purée the tomatoes in the blender, leaving a little texture. Heat 2 tbsp of olive oil in a saucepan and cook 1 finely chopped onion until soft. Add tomatoes and cook until all the extra water evaporates. Season with salt and sugar.

to assemble

Now add this sauce to the corn and cottage cheese mixture and mix well. Grease a 1 litre casserole or baking dish with butter and pour this mixture into it. Bake in a preheated oven at 375°F for 10 minutes. Remove from the oven and garnish will dollops of sour cream and serve immediately.

Note Crisp corn tortillas go extremely well with this baked dish.

MEXICAN CHEESE FONDUE

ingredients

225 gms	Monterey Jack cheese (grated)
225 gms	Sharp Cheddar cheese (grated)
2 tbsp	Corn flour
2 cups	White wine
5 tbsp	Chunky salsa
1 tbsp	Taco seasoning
2	Jalapeño peppers (chopped)
1 tsp	Butter
1 clove	Garlic (crushed)

To Serve
Tortilla Chips

method

Place fondue dish on the gas, melt butter and add garlic. Let it sizzle and add the wine. Mix both the cheeses and corn flour. Add taco seasoning and salt. Toss it lightly. When the wine starts boiling, add salsa, peppers and boil it further for a minute. Start adding cheese little by little and mix it in a figure of 8 to avoid sticking to the bottom. Continue till all the cheese is incorporated. Simmer on the gas and keep stirring till the fondue is smooth and free of any lumps. You may use a hand beater if you wish. Transfer the dish to the burner at the table and serve hot with tortilla chips.

Serves 6-8

Mexican Vegetable Rice

ingredients

1½ cups	Rice, washed and soaked for ½ an hour
3	Vegetable cubes
1	Large onion, chopped
2 cloves	Garlic, minced
3 cups	Boiling water
250 gms	Peas, carrots and corn
1½ cups	Tomatoes, peeled, deseeded and chopped
3 tbsp	Salad oil
	Salt and Pepper to taste

method

In a wide frying pan, heat the oil over medium heat; add onion, garlic and rice. Cook, stirring until onions are limp and the rice is opaque. Stir in the salt pepper and vegetable cubes dissolved in boiling water. Bring to a boil, cover and simmer for about 20 minutes or until all the liquid is absorbed. Add the peas, carrots, corn and tomatoes. Cook over low heat, stirring just until the vegetables are heated. Serve hot.

Note If you like your rice to be spicy, add 2 red chillies soaked and crushed along with the tomatoes.

CORN AND BEAN BURRITOS

ingredients

4	Flour tortillas
½ cup	Monterey Jack cheese
250 gms	Refried beans
100 gms	Tinned corn kernels
1	Tomato, chopped
½ cup	Shredded lettuce
½ cup	Spicy salsa
2	Green onions, chopped
2	Green chillies, chopped
2 tbsp	Burritos seasoning mix

To Serve
Sour Cream

method

Mix both the cheeses; mix seasoning with refried beans. Mix all the chopped salad. Mix the corn and chillies. Place the warmed tortilla on a plate. Arrange beans, cheeses, corn and salad in layers. Sprinkle with salsa fold each tortilla over, arrange in a baking dish and bake in a hot oven 375°F for 20 minutes. Serve hot with chilled sour cream on the side.

Serves 4

Lebanese food combines the sophistication of European cuisine with the excitement of Eastern spices and is recognised internationally as Arabic. Although food varies from country to country, it is similar throughout the Middle East.

Many traditional Lebanese dishes are simple presentations based on grains and vegetables. Often, the same ingredients are used over and over in different ways in each dish. The combinations of yogurt, cheese, chick pea, vegetables and sesame, offer harmonious blends in numerous assorted medleys. Parsley, mint, garlic and lemons are also widely used. Pastries stuffed with vegetables or nuts, salty or sweet, make for artistic presentations and contrasting textures. Arabic bread, popularly known as 'Pita' either the thick or thin variety, is a must at a Lebanese meal. Let's explore the vegetarian version of this ancient cuisine. Deliciously different, not too complicated, not too expensive and its great for entertaining.

Lebanese Cuisine

Hummus
Chick Pea Dip

ingredients

¼ kg	Chick peas
3-4 tbsp	Tahina paste
3-4 tbsp	Lemon juice
6-8 cloves	Garlic
2-3 sprigs	Parsley or Basil
	Salt to taste

To Serve
Crisp pita bread triangles

To Garnish
Olive oil and chilli powder

method

Soak chick peas for 6 hours with a pinch of soda. Cook it in the pressure cooker until very soft. Remove from the cooker, let it cool down and set aside with the extra water from the cooker. When cooled, put the chick peas in the food processor along with a little water, tahina paste, salt, lemon juice and garlic. Add parsley or basil sprigs for herbed hummus. Churn it till it becomes a thick paste, if you find it a little dry add the water kept in the cooker (3-4 tbsp). Remove from the food processor into a serving bowl and at this point taste it and adjust the salt and lemon flavour to your taste. With a fork make a design on the surface and pour olive oil and sprinkle the chilli powder on top. Serve at room temperature with crisp pita bread.

Serves 6-8

TABBOULEH
Parsley and Mint Salad

ingredients

½ cup	Fine grained cracked wheat
½ cup	Finely chopped onion
½ tsp	All spice powder
½ tsp	Pepper
1 tsp	Salt
3 cups	Finely chopped parsley
½ cup	Finely chopped scallions
2 cups	Finely chopped tomatoes
½ cup	Chopped mint leaves (optional)
½ cup	Fresh lemon juice
¾ cup	Olive oil

method

Rinse the cracked wheat several times then cover with water, topping it by half an inch. Let it soak for 20 minutes, then drain it well, squeezing out all the excess water. Combine the minced onion with the all spice powder, pepper and salt. Set aside. In a large bowl, combine the parsley, scallions, tomatoes and mint. Gently fold in the drained wheat and refrigerate until an hour before serving. Just before serving, stir in the seasoned onion and dress it with lemon juice and oil to taste.

BABA GANNOUSH
Eggplant Dip

ingredients

1 large	Eggplant, roasted
1	Onion, minced
4-5 cloves	Garlic (paste)
3 tbsp	Tahina paste
3 tbsp	Thick yogurt
½ tsp	Mustard
	Salt and sugar to taste

To Serve
Crisp pita bread triangles

To Garnish
Olive oil and chopped olives

method

To roast the eggplant, wash and dry, prick with a fork or knife and then apply oil over it and place on the gas or on charcoal if you wish, turning it from time to time until it is completely soft. Remove from the gas and take off the skin and mash the eggplant with a fork. Add onion, garlic, tahina, salt, pepper, mustard and yogurt. Place this mixture in a wide serving bowl or a deep plate, smoothen the surface and dribble olive oil and chopped olives on the top. Serve at room temperature with crisp pita bread.

Opposite (clockwise)
i) Crisp Pita Bread ii) Batata Hara
iii) Baba Ganoush iv) Hummus

FALAFEL
Green Bean Rissoles

ingredients

¼ kg	Green moong daal
3 tbsp	Chopped coriander
3	Green chillies, chopped
2	Onions, chopped
2 cloves	Garlic,crushed
½ tsp	Baking powder
1 tsp	Zatar spice mix
	Oil for deep frying
	Salt to taste

To Serve
Hot Sauce and Tahina Sauce (recipe follows)

method

Soak the dal in water overnight. Grind it in a liquidiser along with the chillies, garlic and coriander leaves, into a thick paste. Add salt. Just before frying add finely chopped onions, zatar mix and baking powder. Beat well before frying. Take 2 spoons of the mixture onto your hand, flatten it with your fingertips and fry 8-10 pieces at a time in hot oil over a medium flame, in hot oil. Serve hot with Hot Sauce, Tahina Sauce or use them to fill falafel sandwiches.

Opposite (clockwise)
i) Fattoush ii) Falafal   iii) Falafel Sandwiches
iv) Hot Sauce v) Tahina Sauce

**Makes approx.
20 rissoles**

HOT SAUCE

ingredients

4	Ripe red tomatoes
10	Dry red chillies (soaked)
5 cloves	Garlic
½ tsp	Lemon juice
	Salt to taste

method

Place the tomatoes in hot water and remove the skins and chop the tomatoes. Mix with chillies, garlic, lemon juice and salt. Blend these in the liquidiser and set aside.

Makes 1 cup

TAHINA SAUCE

ingredients

3 tbsp	Tahina paste
2	Green chillies
½ tsp	Mustard powder
4-6 tbsp	Yogurt
	Salt and sugar to taste

method

Blend all the ingredients together in a liquidiser, add a little ice water if necessary. Set aside.

Makes ½ cup

FALAFEL SANDWICHES

ingredients

5 pieces	Pita bread cut into half and slit
20 pieces	Falafel
1½ cups	salad

To Serve
Hot Sauce and Tahina sauce

For the Salad

3	Tomatoes, finely chopped
3	Spring onion, finely chopped
¼ kg	White cabbage, finely chopped
	Salt to taste

method

For the Salad
Mix all the ingredients together and set aside.

Makes 1½ cups

how to proceed

Slightly, heat the pita bread in the oven. Place salad at the bottom of the slit pita. Top with falafel, hot sauce, tahina sauce, some more salad and some more of the two sauces. Serve immediately.

MUHAMMARA
Roasted Red Pepper Dip

ingredients

200 gms	Red peppers, roasted
¼ cup	Fresh breadcrumbs
$1/_3$ cup	Walnuts or pine nuts, lightly toasted and finely chopped
2-3 large cloves	Garlic, made into a paste with 1 tsp salt
1 tbsp	Lemon juice
2 tbsp	Pomegranate juice
1 tbsp	Raw sugar
1 tsp	Cumin ground
½ tsp	Hot dried red chilli flakes
¼ cup	Extra virgin olive oil
	Salt to taste

To serve
Crisp pita bread triangles

method

In a food processor blend together all the ingredients except olive oil until the mixture is smooth and with the motor running, add the oil gradually. Transfer the muhammara into a bowl and serve at room temperature with crisp pita triangles.

Makes about 1¾ cups

FATAYER BIJIBN
Cheese Pies

ingredients

12	Wonton wrappers
¼ kg	Feta cheese or goat cheese
1 tsp	Chopped basil
2 cloves	Garlic, minced
1 tsp	Corn flour
	A little corn flour paste
	Oil for frying

method

Grate or mash the feta cheese, add basil, garlic, salt and corn flour. Mix well. Now take one wonton wrapper at a time, cut it diagonally and make a triangle. Now fold each triangle like a cone and stuff with one teaspoon of cheese and then close it with the help of corn flour paste. Seal well. Set aside. Make all the rest the same way and fry just before serving. Drain well on kitchen paper and serve hot.

BATTATA HARA
Hot Spicy Potatoes

ingredients

500 gms	New potatoes, diced and half boiled
3-4 tbsp	Olive oil
2-3	Hot red chillies, finely chopped
3 cloves	Garlic, crushed
1 bunch	Fresh coriander, finely chopped
	Oil for frying

method

Fry diced potatoes in oil until crispy and cooked. Place on a kitchen towel to dry. Heat the oil in a large pan. Add chillies and garlic, cook for a minute or two. Add potatoes, salt and coriander and cook gently, stirring until it wilts. Serve hot with toothpicks. You may also add 1 tsp each of cumin and coriander powder, along with chillies.

Serves 6

PISTACHIO DIP

ingredients

1 cup	Thick yogurt, hung and sieved
2	Green onions, finely chopped
3-4 cloves	Garlic, crushed
8-10	Small pistachios, shelled
1 tbsp	Finely chopped coriander
1 tbsp	Lemon juice
	Salt to taste

To Serve
Potato wafers, crudité or crisp pita bread

method

Put all the ingredients and half the yogurt into a grinder and blend well. Remove and mix with remaining yogurt. Pour into a serving bowl and chill until ready to serve. Crudités should also be chilled before serving.

Makes 1½ cups

FATAYER BI SABANIKH
Spinach Pies

ingredients

250 gms	Puff pastry dough
450 gms	Spinach leaves, cleaned, washed, dried, chopped and shredded
4 tbsp	Olive oil
3 tbsp	Raisins (optional)
1	Onion, finely chopped
100 gms	Coarsely chopped walnuts
½ tsp	All spice powder
100 gms	Feta or Cheddar cheese
	A little plain flour for rolling
	Juice of 2 lemons
	Salt, pepper and nutmeg to taste

method

Heat 2 tbsp of olive oil, cook the spinach till it crumples to a soft mass. Remove from heat and cool. In a bowl, mix the rest of the ingredients. Add spinach and mix well. Set aside. Roll out ½ the dough very lightly into a long strip. Cut into 2-3 inch squares. Take one square, put 1 tbsp of filling over it, in one corner, leaving a little border around. Cover with the other half and seal with the help of water. Lightly brush with oil. Make all the pastries like this. Place them on a greased baking tray and bake at 350°F for 20 minutes until lightly browned.

Serves 6-8

MANAQUISH
Spiced Pita Bread

ingredients

4 pieces	Pita bread
2 tbsp	Olive oil
1 tbsp	Zatar spice mix
1 tsp	Lemon juice

method

Mix together olive oil, zatar and lemon juice. Set aside. Slightly toast pita bread, when it is hot, apply oil mixture to cover the bread and toast for 1 minute again. Cut it into pieces as per your liking and serve hot as a snack or an appetizer.

FATTOUSH
Bread Salad

ingredients

1	Pita bread
3-4	Firm tomatoes, chopped
1 head	Iceberg lettuce, cut into square pieces
1 bunch	Parsley, finely chopped
2 tbsp	Finely chopped fresh mint
3 tbsp	Finely chopped fresh coriander
2 cloves	Garlic, crushed
6 tbsp	Olive oil
1 tsp	Powdered dry pomegranate seeds
	Juice of 2 lemons
	Salt and pepper to taste

To Garnish
A handful of toasted pine nuts

method

Open out pita bread and toast till crisp and brown, then crunch it in your hands to break into little pieces. Put these pieces into a bowl and moisten this with a little lemon juice, set aside. Mix all the other ingredients in a large salad bowl and refrigerate until ready to use. Just before serving mix toasted bread pieces. Toss the salad gently, garnish with nuts and serve.

Serves 4-6

Italian cuisine is said to be the mother cuisine of southern Europe. Italians believe that preserving the characteristic tastes of the separate ingredients rather than blending them together, enhances the pleasure of eating. Things have to be good in themselves, without aid. A dish of pasta is only as good as the pasta itself. The Italian menu is lively and interesting and has a wide variety of foods for vegetarians. It ranges from rich, stomach-warming soups to dazzling anti pasti and salads, crusty breads and a variety of pasta cooked perfectly soft but *al dente* (that is, slightly resistant to bite) and, a special variety of rice known as *Arborio*, as well as a profusion of delicious cakes, cheeses and ice creams.

Italians generously add taste to their food with a wide variety of fresh or dried herbs, spices and more importantly, olives, either by themselves or as olive oil. The best olive oils in the world are from Italy. There is a medley of fine vegetables used in Italian food and their variety of tomato is the staple ingredient. It is at its best in simple salads and is used extensively in most Italian dishes and sauces. The small, sweet red variety of tomatoes is the best in the world.

The Italian masterpieces like their ice creams and melt-in-the-mouth desserts such as Tiramisu, are exquisite cooling finales to the warming meals.

ITALIAN CUISINE

MINESTRONE SOUP

ingredients

For the Soup

¼ kg	Dried white beans (soaked overnight)
2 oz(50 gms)	Butter
450 gms	Green peas, unshelled
225 gms	Zucchini, diced
250 gms	Carrots, diced
150 gms	Potatoes, diced
50 gms	Celery, thinly sliced
2	Onions, finely chopped
100 gms	Leek, finely chopped
3	Large tomatoes, coarsely chopped
3 pints	Vegetable stock
1 tsp	Salt
250 gms	Rice or pasta, cooked
	1 bay leaf and 2 parsley sprigs, tied together
	Freshly ground pepper

To Garnish

¾ tbsp	Finely chopped basil
¾ tbsp	Finely chopped parsley
2 tbsp	Finely chopped garlic

To Serve

2 oz(50 gms)	Freshly grated Parmesan cheese

method

Boil beans until tender and set aside. Melt ½ the butter over moderate heat, then add the peas, zucchini, carrots, potatoes and celery, tossing constantly with a wooden spoon for 2-3 minutes.
Set aside.

In a large 6 quart soup pot, melt the rest of the butter and stir in the onion and leek. Fry for 7-8 minutes or until soft. Stir in the tomatoes and vegetables that were cooked earlier, the stock, the bay leaf and parsley sprigs, salt and pepper. Bring the soup to a boil over high heat and simmer for 25 minutes. Remove and discard the bay leaf and parsley, add cooked pasta or rice and white beans. Cook for 20 minutes more. Adjust the seasoning. Garnish with herbs and garlic. Serve hot with Parmesan cheese separately.

Serves 8-10

GARLIC AND HERB BREAD

ingredients

6	Oblong breads
100 gms	Butter
1 tsp	Minced garlic
1 tsp	Freshly chopped herbs
1 tsp	Salt

method

Beat butter with a wooden spoon, add garlic, herbs and salt, set aside. Cut the bread at a slant making half an inch thick slices. Ensure the bread remains together, that is, don't cut it all the way through. Wrap it in foil and bake for 10 minutes.

Makes 18 pieces

Bagna Cauda
Hot Cheese and Garlic Dip

ingredients

For the Dip

200 gms	Fresh cream
2 tbsp	Butter
2 tbsp	Chopped garlic
50 gms	Grated cheese mixed with 1 tsp flour

To Serve

1	Cucumber, peeled, deseeded and cut into 2 inch pieces
2	Carrots, peeled, and cut into 2 inch pieces
1	Green pepper, deseeded and cut into 2 inch pieces
4 sticks	Celery, cut into 2 inch pieces
1 bunch	Spring onions, trimmed and cut into 2 inch pieces
12	Cherry tomatoes
100 gms	Fresh mushrooms, whole if small, quartered if large
1 pkt	Baby corn
1	White radish, skinned and cut into 2 inch pieces
8-10	Italian bread sticks
	A small head of lettuce, broken into separate leaves

method

Soak the vegetables in a bowl of ice cubes and water to crispen them. Pat dry and cover with foil and refrigerate. Bring the cream to a boil and set aside. Get a flame proof casserole dish and melt the butter in it. Add garlic, fry for 1 minute. Add the cream, cheese and flour mixture. Simmer, stirring continuously. Serve at once with cold vegetables and bread sticks.

Note 1 tbsp of freshly chopped herbs, added with garlic also gives a good change.

Opposite (clockwise)
i) Garlic and Herb Bread ii) Parmesan Cheese
iii) Aglio Olio Pasta iv) Pesto Sauce v) Marinara Sauce
vi) Cheese Sauce vii) Nepolitan Salad Bowl

BRUSCHETTA

ingredients

2 large	Tomatoes
½ tsp each	Salt and pepper
2 large	Basil leaves, finely chopped
1 tbsp	Olive oil
1 clove	Garlic (optional)
1 tsp	Paprika
1 small	French bread, sliced and lightly toasted
2 tbsp	Parmesan cheese

method

Cut the tomatoes into small chunks. Mince garlic, basil and paprika together in a bowl. Add olive oil, chopped tomatoes, salt and pepper. Refrigerate for 2 hours. When you wish to serve, remove the mixture from the fridge, spoon onto each slice of bread, top it with Parmesan and serve as an appetizer.

Opposite (clockwise)
i) Chilli Oil ii) Mushroom Cocktail iii) Bruschetta
iv) Hot Cheese Garlic Dip (Bagna Cauda)

Pesto Pinwheels

ingredients

1 loaf	White bread
1 cup	Pesto sauce
½ cup	Roasted and chopped red bell peppers

To Serve
¼ cup Parmesan cheese

method

Cut the bread into 5 horizontal slices, discard the edges. Place one long slice on a board, spread $^1/_5$ cup of pesto evenly on it, sprinkle 1½ tbsp of the red peppers on it and roll the bread tightly, securing the edge with a toothpick. Repeat this for all the slices. Place all the rolls on a tray and cover with a wet cloth. Chill for 15-20 minutes. When chilled, slice the rolls into ½ inch circles. Arrange them on a serving plate, sprinkle with Parmesan and serve.

Serves 6-8

Pesto Sauce

ingredients

1 tbsp	Finely chopped garlic
1 ½ cups	Fresh basil leaves, stripped from their stems
1 tsp	Salt
2 tsp	Black pepper
5 tsp	Chopped walnuts or pine nuts
1 cup	Olive oil or corn oil
50 gms	Parmesan cheese, freshly grated

method

In a blender, combine basil, salt, pepper, garlic, walnuts or pine nuts and oil. Blend them at high speed until the ingredients are smooth. The sauce should be thin enough to run off the spatula easily. Transfer the sauce to a bowl and stir in the grated cheese. Serve the pesto thoroughly mixed into hot drained and tossed pasta with soft butter.

LAYERED PIZZA DIP

ingredients

1 cup (8oz)	Soft cream cheese with onion and chives
½ cup	Chunky pizza sauce
½ cup	Chopped green peppers
¼ cup	Finely chopped olives
2 tbsp	Finely chopped basil
1 cup	Pizza cheese (Mozzarella + Cheddar)

To Serve
Thin pizza base, cut into triangles and toasted

method

Preheat the oven to 350°F. In a 9″ pie dish layer all the ingredients in the order listed. Bake for 10-15 minutes, until the cheese has melted. Serve warm with toasted pizza bread.

Serves 6-8

Sweet Pepper Pinwheels

ingredients

4	Large peppers
4 cloves	Garlic, crushed
$^1/_3$ cup	Chopped basil
8 thin slices	Cheese
10	Chopped, large olives
1 stick	Chopped celery
1 tbsp	Red wine vinegar
	Olive oil for dribbling
	Salt and pepper to taste

method

Line a baking tray with foil. Wash and dry the peppers, place them on the try and roast them in a hot oven till soft and slightly burnt. Remove from the oven, place them in a plastic bag, close the bag and shake it till all the air has been removed. Remove from the bag. Cool and cut the peppers into halves, remove the stems and let them cool completely. In a small bowl, mix together olives, celery, garlic, vinegar, salt and pepper. Toss till mixed. Cut the cheese slices to the size of the pepper halves. Place them over the pepper, spoon the mixture over the cheese and roll the pepper slice. Lock it with the help of a toothpick. Repeat for the rest of the pepper slices. Chill thoroughly. Just before serving, slice them like pinwheels and serve.

PIZZA PUFF

ingredients

½ kg	Puff pastry dough
1 cup	Marinara (pizza) sauce
½ cup	Mozzarella + Cheddar cheese
	Olive oil to brush

To Garnish
2 tbsp dried mixed herbs mixed with red pepper

method

Roll out the puff pastry dough to about ½ inch thick. Cut it into 3" x 3" squares. Spoon 2 tbsp of pizza sauce in the centre of the square, sprinkle 1 tbsp of cheese and put water on all the edges of the square. Pick up the two opposite corners and lightly press them together to form a triangle. Brush with olive oil, place them on a baking tray and bake in a moderate oven for 20-25 minutes or until golden brown. Sprinkle with herb seasoning and serve.

Makes 12 puffs

OLIVE AND CHEESE SQUARES

ingredients

½ cup	Finely chopped ripe olives
2 cups	Finely grated sharp cheddar cheese
2 tbsp	Mayonnaise
2	Green onions, finely chopped
½ tsp	Salt
12 slices	Whole wheat bread, cut into quarters with the crust removed

To Garnish
A few pepper strips

method

In a medium sized bowl, combine olives, cheese, mayonnaise, onions and salt. Set aside. Preheat the oven to 150°C. Lightly toast the bread. Spread about 2 tbsp of the olive mixture over each slice. Arrange the squares on an ungreased baking sheet. Bake until the topping bubbles i.e. for 4-5 minutes. Serve hot.

Makes 48 squares

SUNDRIED TOMATO AIOLI DIP WITH CRUDITÉS

ingredients

3 cloves	Garlic, peeled and halved
¼ tsp	Salt
6	Sun dried tomatoes, soaked in water for half an hour
2 tbsp	Olive oil
2 tbsp	Coarsely chopped pine nuts
1 cup	Cottage cheese
$\frac{1}{3}$ cup	Thick yogurt
¼ cup	Mayonnaise

To Serve
Freshly cut vegetables, such as broccoli, baby corn, asparagus, carrots, cucumber, celery etc.

method

Place the garlic on a cutting board and sprinkle with salt. Using the flat side of a knife, crush the garlic, add the sun dried tomatoes to it and mince to a coarse paste. Purée the cottage cheese in the processor, add the yogurt and mayonnaise and blend well. Add the garlic paste, blend well. Season with salt. Transfer it into a serving bowl. Sprinkle with olive oil and pine nuts. Serve with raw vegetables.

Serves 10

Caesar Dip With Crudités

ingredients

For the Dip

½ cup	Mayonnaise
½ cup	Thick curd
¼ cup	Fresh cream, beaten
1 tbsp	Lemon juice
1 clove	Garlic, pressed
½ tsp	Mustard powder
½ cup	Grated Parmesan or Cheddar cheese
	Salt and pepper to taste

To Serve

A few lettuce leaves
Assorted fresh vegetables
Toasted bread sticks

method

Mix the first 7 ingredients in a bowl, season with salt and pepper and keep chilled until ready to serve. Serve with the vegetables or bread sticks. A special way to serve this dip, is to wrap the lettuce leaf around the bread stick and then dip, so you really get the feel of having Caesar's Salad.

Mushroom Cocktail

ingredients

250 gms	Mushrooms, cut into quarters
¼ cup	Spring onions, thinly sliced
¼ cup	Olive oil
3 tbsp	Water
2 cloves	Garlic, crushed
1	Medium sized tomato, finely chopped
1 tbsp each	Basil and parsley, finely chopped
	Juice of one lemon
	Salt and pepper to taste

To Garnish
A few lettuce leaves

method

In a medium sized bowl mix together oil, water, lemon juice, crushed garlic, spring onions, tomatoes, herbs, salt and pepper. Mix well. Then toss the mushrooms in this mixture and chill for 3-4 hours. Serve cold on a bed of lettuce.

Serves 4-6

Caesar's Salad

ingredients

2 heads	Iceberg lettuce
1 cup	Bread croutons
¼ cup	Cheese, cut into small cubes
¼ cup	Hard boiled egg (optional)
½ cup	Caesar dressing (recipe follows)

For the Dressing

1	Egg
1	Juice of 1 lemon
½ tsp	Worcestershire sauce
1 tsp each	Salt and pepper
2 cloves	Garlic
¼ cup	Olive or salad oil
1 tsp	Mustard

method

For the Caesar Dressing

Ease the egg into boiling water and boil exactly for 1 minute, then crack it into a bowl, breaking it up with a fork. Add all the ingredients for the dressing and mix well.

To Toss the Salad

Place washed square pieces of lettuce in a bowl with the dressing and toss lightly. Arrange croutons, cheese and boiled egg on top and serve at once.

For Eggless Dressing

Mix together ½ cup thick yogurt, 1 tbsp lemon juice, 1 tsp Worcestershire sauce, 1 tsp sugar, 1 tsp salt, 1 tsp pepper, 2 cloves crushed garlic, ½ cup beaten fresh cream and 1 tsp mustard. Chill this for 1 hour before using.

Nepolitan Salad Bowl

ingredients

For the Salad

4	Medium sized tomatoes, quartered
1	Small green pepper, thinly sliced
1	Small red pepper, thinly sliced
1 head	Lettuce, washed and shredded
4 oz (100gms)	Sweet corn, boiled
2 oz (50gms)	Mozzarella cheese, chopped
3	Hard boiled eggs, sliced (optional)
6	Olives, halved
1 tbsp	Chopped fresh basil leaves
½ cup	Vinaigrette dressing (recipe follows)

For the Vinaigrette Dressing

3 tbsp	Vinegar
3 tbsp	Water
1 clove	Garlic, minced
1 tsp	Mustard
1 tsp	Salt
½ tsp	Pepper
½ tsp	Oregano, dried/fresh
½ cup	Olive oil

method

For the Salad

Prepare all the vegetables as described above, transfer them into a large bowl and refrigerate until ready to use. They should be chilled for a minimum of 2-3 hours. When you wnat to serve, dribble the dressing over the salad, toss gently and serve at once.

For the Dressing

Mix all the ingredients in a screw top jar. Cover the top tightly and shake vigorously to mix well. Use as required.

Note This dressing keeps well in the refrigerator for 2-3 weeks.

Serves 4-6

Panzanella Salad

ingredients

450 gms	Ripe tomatoes, thinly sliced
1	Red onion, thinly sliced
115 gms	Mozzarella cheese, thinly sliced
1 tbsp	Shredded fresh basil leaves
½ cup	Olive oil
3 tbsp	Wine or Balsamic vinegar
	Juice of 1 lemon
	Salt and pepper to taste

To Garnish
Sliced olives and a bunch of basil leaves

method

Soak the onion slices in cold water for 10 minutes while you prepare the other things. Drain and set aside. Layer the tomatoes, cheese, onions, and basil, seasoning well in between each layer. Sprinkle with oil, vinegar and lemon juice. Top with olives. Cover with cling film and chill until ready to serve.

BEAN SOUP WITH PASTA
Zuppa Di Fagiolo Con La Pasta

ingredients

200 gms	Dried white haricot beans, soaked overnight
8 cups	Water
2 tbsp	Olive oil
250 gms	Tomatoes, blanched and chopped into small cubes
1	Leek, finely chopped
1	Small onion, finely chopped
1 stick	Celery, finely chopped
2 cloves	Garlic, finely chopped
1	Carrot, cut into cubes
1 tsp	Salt
½ cup	Spaghetti, cut into 1" pieces
1 tsp	Dried Italian seasoning
2-3 tbsp	Parmesan cheese
	Freshly ground black pepper

method

In a medium sized saucepan, bring 6 cups of water to a boil and add the soaked beans. Boil for 15 minutes. Drain the beans and set aside. In a large pan, heat the oil. Then, add leek, onion, celery, garlic and half of the tomatoes. Stirring frequently, cook the vegetables for about 10 minutes. Add the water alongwith the beans, salt, carrots, zucchini, pepper and the seasoning and let it simmer over a low flame. Now, add the spaghetti and let it simmer for 10-15 minutes, until the pasta is tender. Adjust the seasoning. Serve hot with grated cheese in individual bowls and hot garlic toast.

For the Garlic Toast

Spread 6-8 one-inch thick slices of bread on a greased baking sheet and bake in preheated (350°F, Gas Mark 3) oven for 15 minutes. Mix 2-3 tbsp olive oil, 1½ tsp finely chopped garlic and 1 tsp dried herbs. Apply this mixture on both sides of each slice and bake again until browned.

Serves 6

PASTA SALAD WITH SUNDRIED TOMATOES

ingredients

For the Salad

1 cup	Farfalle/Conchiegelle pasta
3	Spring onions, finely chopped
¼ cup	Sun dried tomatoes, soaked and cut into strips
½ cup	Peas and corn, boiled
1 tbsp	Fresh oregano leaves
2 tbsp	Chopped basil leaves
1 cup	Cleaned and shredded fresh spinach leaves

To Garnish

4 tbsp	Pine nuts, toasted

For the Dressing

¼ cup	Olive oil
2 tbsp	Wine vinegar
1 tsp	Balsamic vinegar
1 clove	Garlic, crushed
1 tsp	Raw sugar
	Salt and pepper to taste

method

Cook the pasta in a large pan of boiling water until tender. Drain, and then rinse in cold water and transfer to a large salad bowl. Add the onions, tomatoes, peas, corn and spinach, oregano and basil to the pasta and chill until ready to serve.

To make the dressing, combine all the ingredients in a screw-top jar and shake well until combined. Set aside. Just before serving, pour the dressing over the salad, toss well and garnish with pine nuts.

Serves 4-6

BALSAMIC POTATO SALAD

ingredients

500 gms	Baby potatoes
¾ cup	Sour cream (½ cup thick yogurt, ¼ cup fresh cream and 1 tbsp of lemon juice)
2 tbsp	Balsamic vinegar
1 tbsp	Olive oil
2 tsp	Salt
½ tsp	Pepper
½ cup	Spring onions, sliced
¼ cup	Coarsely chopped celery
2 tbsp	Pine nuts, toasted

To Garnish
A few lettuce leaves

method

Cook the potatoes in a large pot of salted water over medium heat, just until tender for about 15-20 minutes. In the meanwhile, make the balsamic dressing. Whisk the sour cream, balsamic vinegar, olive oil, salt and pepper in a large bowl until blended. Stir in all except 2 tbsp of the spring onions. Drain the potatoes, remove the skin and transfer to the bowl. Add the dressing and gently toss to coat. Add celery and toss again. Line the serving bowl with lettuce leaves and spoon the salad into it. Sprinkle the reserved spring onions and pine nuts over it.

Serves 6

PEPPERONATA
Braised Sweet Peppers With Tomatoes And Onions

ingredients

1 tbsp	Butter
2 tbsp	Corn or olive oil
1 ½ cups	Slice onions
450 gms	Mixed peppers, peeled, deseeded and cut into 1 inch strips.
450 gms	Tomatoes, peeled, deseeded and coarsely chopped
1 tsp	Vinegar
1 tsp	Salt
	Freshly ground black pepper

method

In a heavy skillet, melt butter with oil over moderate heat. Add the onions and cook them turning them frequently, until they are soft and lightly browned. Stir in the peppers. Reduce the heat, cover and cook for 10 minutes. Add the tomatoes, vinegar, salt and pepper cover and cook for 5 more minutes stirring gently. Continue until almost all the liquid has boiled away. Serve the Pepperonata as a hot vegetable dish with the main course or as a cold antipasto.

Barbecued Pizza

ingredients

For the Dough

1¼ cups	Plain flour or Whole wheat flour
2 tbsp	Dry yeast
½ cup	Tepid water
2 tsp	Whole sugar
1 tbsp	Olive oil
½ tsp	Salt

For the Topping

1 cup	Thick pizza sauce
1	Medium sized onion, finely chopped
1	Medium sized capsicum, finely chopped
200 gms	Pizza cheese, grated
10-12	Basil leaves, finely chopped

To Serve

Crushed red pepper

method

To make the dough, sieve the flour in a bowl with salt. In a small bowl, take tepid water and sprinkle yeast and sugar over it. Cover and place in a closed cupboard for 10 minutes. When the liquid is frothy, pour over the sieved flour and oil, making a soft dough. Add a little extra water if required. Cover it and keep for 1-1½ hours in a closed oven or until the dough has doubled in size. When you want to serve, punch down the dough and divide into 8 small parts. Take one portion and with the help of dry flour, roll it into a 3" diametre round. Place this on the grill of gas top tandoor or in the oven at 150ºc. and cook for 3-4 minutes. Turn it over and cook for another 2 minutes. Now remove from the grill and spread 1½ tbsp of thick sauce evenly on the round. Sprinkle with onion, capsicum, basil and cheese. Grill again until the cheese melts and serve immediately.

Aglio Olio Pasta

ingredients

8 oz(200gms)	Packaged pasta
3 tbsp	Olive oil
6 large cloves	Garlic, crushed
1 tbsp	Chopped basil
	Salt, black pepper and
	Crushed red pepper to taste
	Salted boiling water

method

Boil the pasta in salted water until soft but firm. Then drain and place under running cold water. Drain all the water out. In a large frying pan heat olive oil, then add garlic, basil, crushed red pepper and fry it for two minutes on a medium flame. Add drained pasta, salt and pepper. Serve hot pasta by itself or accompanied by any of the pasta sauces.

Serves 4

Gnocchi Alla Romana
Semolina Dumplings Baked with Butter and Cheese

ingredients

2½ cups	Milk
1½ tsp	Salt
2	Eggs, lightly beaten
½ cup	Semolina
½ cup	Grated cheese (Gouda + Cheddar)
¼ cup	Parmesan cheese freshly grated
50 gms	Butter, melted
	A pinch of ground nutmeg
	Freshly ground black pepper

method

Butter a 9" inch round or 8"x 8" square baking dish and set aside. In a heavy saucepan bring the milk, salt, nutmeg and a few grindings of pepper to a boil over moderate heat. Add semolina gradually, so that the milk never stops boiling, stirring constantly with a wooden spoon. Continue cooking and stirring until thick. Remove the pan from heat and let it cool completely. Mix ½ cup of cheese to lightly beaten eggs and add this to the semolina mixture. Blend well. Apply a little oil on your palms, take 1 tbsp of mixture and lightly roll it in your hand and place the rolls on a greased baking dish. Dribble melted butter over the gnocchi, sprinkle Parmesan cheese and bake in a hot oven 400° F, for 15 minutes and serve at once with tomato or pesto sauce.

Serves 4-6

PASTA WITH CHEESE
AND MARINARA SAUCE

ingredients

For the Pasta

8 oz	Packaged pasta
3 tbsp	Olive oil
6 large cloves	Garlic, crushed
1 tbsp	Chopped basil
	Salt, black pepper and crushed red pepper
	Salted boiling water

For the Cheese Sauce

2 tbsp	Butter
2 tbsp	Plain flour
1 cup	Milk
1 cup	Cream
2 tbsp	Parmesan cheese
	A dash of nutmeg
	Salt, pepper and mustard to taste

For the Marinara Sauce

2 tbsp	Olive oil
2 medium	Onions, finely chopped
1 large	Carrot, grated
1 large	Green pepper, finely chopped
4 cloves	Garlic, minced
1 kg	Tomatoes, blanched and chopped.
1 pkt	Tomato purée
2 tbsp	Salt
½ tbsp	Pepper
1 tbsp	Mixed herbs, dried
1	Bay leaf
1 tbsp	Finely chopped basil

method

For the Pasta

Boil the pasta in salted water until soft, then drain and pass under running cold water. Drain all the water out. In a large frying pan, heat olive oil, then add garlic, basil, crushed red pepper and fry for two minutes on a medium flame. Add drained pasta, salt and pepper. Set aside.

Serves 4

For the Cheese Sauce

Melt the butter, add the plain flour and stir for 3-4 minutes. Take it off the heat. Stir in milk gradually. Mix well, making sure that there are no lumps. Return to heat. Add seasoning, bring it to a boil and take it off the heat. Add cream and cheese. Set aside for serving with the pasta.

Makes 2 cups

For the Marinara Sauce

In a saucepan heat olive oil and sauté the onions, carrots, green peppers and garlic. Cook until the vegetables are tender. Add the remaining ingredients and bring to a boil. Remove from heat and set aside. At this point, you could purée half the sauce and mix it up with the rest. Serve hot with the pasta. It is often used as pizza sauce as well.

Note   i)   Keep 1 cup of grated Cheddar cheese to serve with the pasta and the sauces, if you like extra cheese.

          ii) Keep 1 cup of chopped and sautéed mushrooms to serve with the pasta.

Makes 3-4 cups

Fettuccine Al Burro
Flat Noodles With Butter And Cheese

ingredients

125 gms	Butter
50 gms	Double cream
50 gms	Freshly grated Parmesan Cheese
450 gms	Fettuccine (recipe follows)

For the Fettuccine

200 gms	Plain flour
1	Egg
1	Egg white
¾ tbsp	Oil
1 tsp	Salt
3 tbsp	Water
	Additional plain flour for rolling

method

For the Fettuccine

Pour the flour into a large mixing bowl, make a well in the centre, break an egg and add the egg white, oil and salt. Mix together with a fork, until the dough gathers into a rough ball. Moisten dry bits remaining, if any, with drops of water and press them into the ball. Cover with cloth and keep for ½ an hour.

For Making Pasta with a Machine

Pull out 1/3 of the dough at a time. Dust the dough lightly with flour and roll it 4 to 5 times through rollers set furthest apart. When the dough is smooth and elastic, roll it out setting the machine to the second notch and the rollers closer together. Roll a very thin sheet of pasta and for fettuccine cut it through in wide strips. Cook them right away in a large pan of boiling water for 5 minutes or until just tender.

For Making Pasta by Hand

Divide the dough into half. Place 1 ball on a floured surface and flatten it with your hand into an oblong 1" thick. Dust the top lightly with flour using a very heavy rolling pin. Roll in an up and down movement until the dough is paper thin. If the dough sticks, lift carefully and sprinkle more flour under it. To make fettuccine, dust the rolled dough lightly with flour, let it rest for 10 minutes, then gently roll into a jam-roll shape. With a long sharp knife, slice it cross-wise into even strips ¼inch wide. Unroll strips and put aside on grease proof paper. In the same way roll second half and boil in the same way as given above.

For Fettuccine al Burro

While the fettuccine is boiling, place a large serving dish in a hot oven. When the fettuccine has boiled as per method shown above, thoroughly drain and transfer it to the warm serving dish. Cream butter until light and fluffy, beat in cream a little at a time and beat in grated cheese and add this mixture to the fettuccine and toss it until well coated. Taste and season generously with salt and pepper. Serve at once. Serve extra cheese in a separate bowl.

For Eggless Pasta

2 cups plain flour, ½ tsp salt, ½ cup warm water, 1 tbsp oil, ½ tsp baking powder. Make the dough same way as egg pasta, knead for 10 - 15 mins, cover and rest for 20 minutes and make pasta by hand or machine and boil in the same way.

Note You could also use ready packet of fettuccine, if you don't wish to make it at home.

Serves 4-6

ingredients

For the Pasta

5-6 quarts	Water
250 gms	Readymade/home made lasagna
200 gms	Cheddar cheese, grated
50 gms	Parmesan cheese, grated

For the Cream Sauce

3 tbsp	Plain flour
1½ cups	Milk
2 tbsp	Parmesan cheese
200 gms	Cream
	A pinch of ground nutmeg
	Salt and Pepper to taste

For the Marinara Sauce
Please refer to page 129-130

method

Generously butter a 9 x 12 inch serving casserole or baking dish. In a large pot bring water, salt and oil to a bubbling boil on high heat. Add the lasagna, stirring gently for a few moments to prevent the pasta from sticking together. Boil until the lasagna is tender, but *al dente*. Place the pot under cold running water for a few moments to cool the pasta. Then lay the strips side by side on a paper towel to drain. Prepare both sauces.

For the Cream Sauce
In a heavy saucepan, melt the butter over moderate heat and stir in the flour. Remove the pan from the heat and pour in the milk and cream all at once, beating with a wire whisk until the flour is partially dissolved. Return the pan to heat and cook, stirring constantly. When the sauce comes to a boil and thickens into a smooth cream, simmer for 2-3 minutes. Remove from heat and season.

to assemble

Preheat the oven to 350°F. Spread a layer of Cream sauce over the bottom of the casserole dish. Take each strip of Lasagna, place it on the cutting board, put 1 tsp of Cheddar cheese on it and roll. Place the rolls side by side in the baking dish, pour some more Cream Sauce and Marinara sauce alternately over them and finally top with grated Parmesan cheese and bake for 30 minutes.

option

You could also layer the lasagna in another way – spread a layer of cream sauce over the bottom of the casserole or baking dish. Spread over it a layer of Marinara sauce. Lay one third of the lasagna over it, overlapping the strips slightly. Sprinkle grated cheese and repeat the layers of both the sauces, pasta and cheese twice more. Top with grated Parmesan cheese and bake for 30 minutes.

Serves 6-8

PASTA PRIMAVERA

ingredients

1 recipe	Cooked and tossed pasta of your choice
¼ cup	Butter
200 gms	Asparagus, cut into 1" pieces
1 pkt	Mushrooms, washed and sliced
1 medium	Carrot, thinly sliced
1 medium	Zucchini, sliced
½ cup	Green peas, boiled
3 stems	Green onions, sliced with greens
2 tbsp	Freshly chopped basil
1 cup	Fresh cream
¼ cup	Grated parmesan cheese
	Salt, pepper and nutmeg to taste

method

Cook and toss the pasta as per recipe. In a large frying pan, melt the butter and add asparagus, mushrooms, carrot and zucchini. Cook for 3 minutes. Stir occasionally. Cover and cook for 2 more minutes. Add green onions, peas, basil, salt, pepper, nutmeg and cream. Cook until the liquid boils all over in shiny bubbles. Now place the pasta in the pan in which it was cooked and pour the vegetable sauce over it. Mix it gently to coat the pasta. Add most of the Parmesan cheese and mix again. Now remove into a warm serving bowl, sprinkle the rest of the cheese on it and serve immediately.

FETTUCCINI WITH BASIL, FRENCH BEANS AND WALNUTS

ingredients

200 gms	Fresh or dried fettucini
250 gms	French beans, chopped into 1" pieces
½ cup	Walnuts, chopped fine and toasted
3 tbsp	Butter
4 stems	Spring onions, finely chopped
½ cup	Basil leaves, cut into strips
2 cloves	Garlic, finely chopped
1 ½ cups	Vegetable stock
1 ½ cups	Fresh cream or thick milk
	Salt, pepper and chilli flakes to taste

To Garnish
Grated Parmesan cheese

method

Place a large pot of water to boil, with a little salt. In a frying pan, melt butter. Add the green onions and cook over medium heat for 1 minute. Add 2 tbsp of basil, garlic, a pinch of salt and vegetable stock. Cook until the onions are soft. Stir in the fresh cream and cook until slightly thickened. Adjust the salt, pepper and chilli flakes to your liking. When the water boils, add salt and cook the beans for 3-4 minutes or until tender but firm. Scoop them out and add them to the onion-cream mixture. Using the same water, cook the pasta. After it's done, scoop it out and add it to the pan along with the rest of the basil leaves. Keep this warm on a heated plate. Just before serving, toss with walnuts and garnish with Parmesan.

Note Serve with a dry white wine and garlic bread.

BROCCOLI AND PASTA BAKED
WITH CROUTON TOPPING

ingredients

100 gms	Short pasta (such as penne)
500 gms	Broccoli, cut into florets
1	Onions, chopped
2 cloves	Garlic, finely chopped
2 tbsp	Olive oil
4 tsp	Butter
4 tbsp	Flour
4 cup	Milk
1¼ cups	Grated cheese (Cheddar/Parmesan)
½ cup	Freshly shredded basil
5 slices	Day-old bread, crusts removed
50 gms	Butter, melted

method

Cook the pasta in boiling water until tender. Drain and rinse with cold water. Steam the broccoli until tender. Heat the olive oil in a frying pan. Fry the onions and garlic over medium heat until the onions are soft. Add the broccoli and mix well. Take it off the heat. In a large pan, melt the butter, blend in the flour and cook, stirring constantly. Take it off the heat and gradually whisk in the milk. Stir constantly until the mixture boils and thickens. Remove from heat and stir in 1 cup of cheese and the basil. Add the broccoli and onion mixture and the pasta to the sauce and mix thoroughly. Spoon this mixture into a large ovenproof dish. Cut the bread into large cubes, toss them in melted butter and then scatter them over the broccoli mixture. Sprinkle the remaining cheese and bake for 35 minutes, until the top is golden.

Rissotto Alla Milanese

ingredients

6 cups	Vegetable stock
2	Medium onions, finely chopped
100 gms	Butter
450 gms	Uncooked *Arborio* rice
6 tbsp	Dry white wine
100 gms	Fresh asparagus tips or sliced mushrooms
6 tbsp	Freshly grated Parmesan cheese

method

Wash and soak the rice for 10-15 minutes. In a heavy saucepan, melt half the butter and sauté the onions, stirring constantly for about 7-8 minutes. Do not let them turn brown. Stir in the asparagus or mushrooms, and then add the rice and stir for 1 minute. In the meanwhile, keep the stock simmering over a low flame. Add half of this to the rice and cook until the rice is opaque. Pour in the wine and boil until it is completely absorbed. Add the remaining stock and cook further till the rice is tender but not too soft. Stir in the remaining butter and cheese with a fork and serve at once, while the rice is creamy and piping hot!

Serves 6-8

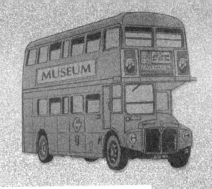

The influence of vegetarian food is spreading rapidly through all the countries of the West. The variety one can find in this kind of food is tremendous. At the same time, this cuisine needs a lot of imagination and technique to achieve perfection, be it cream soups, a variety of salads, baked dishes or appetizers and dips. All these require the artistic side of you to bring out the natural splendour of the ingredients. There are endless possibilities for vegetable combinations whether sautéed, steamed, baked, barbecued or covered with luscious melted cheese, nuts and/or complemented with a rich savoury sauce. Choose and than try out an exciting new recipe and surprise your family and friends.

English Cuisine

Basic Recipe for Cream Soup

ingredients

1 kg	Vegetable of your choice
100 gms	Butter
225 gms	Onions, finely chopped
½ cup	Milk
5 cups	Vegetable stock (recipe follows)
4-5	Vegetable stock cubes (optional)

To Garnish

100 gms	Fresh cream, beaten

method

Cut the vegetables into even sized pieces. Melt the butter in a saucepan, add onions and sauté slowly, until golden. Add milk, vegetables of your choice, salt and pepper or other seasoning according to individual recipes. Cover the pan tightly and place a lid on the saucepan. Simmer on a very low flame for half an hour to one hour depending on the vegetable. When cooked, remove the lid, add stock and liquidise, then pass the mixture through a sieve into a clean pan. Check the seasoning, adjust it to your taste. Garnish with swirls of beaten cream along with individual vegetable garnishes as per the recipe given below and serve.

Serves 10

VEGETABLE STOCK

ingredients

2 tbsp	Oil
4 pieces	Carrot
100 gms	A white pumpkin
4 stalks	Celery
2	Medium sized onions
2	Medium sized tomatoes
100 gms	Mushrooms
2 sprigs	Parsley
3	Peppercorns
1 clove	Garlic
2	Bay leaves
2 tbsp	Salt
2	Vegetable stock cubes

method

Chop all the vegetables into big cubes. Heat the oil in a large pan over moderate heat and add all the ingredients along with 6 cups of water and stir once it comes to a boil. Simmer for 30 minutes. Liquidise and strain into a bowl and set aside until used.

*If you are using this for white stock, exclude tomatoes and add 2 white turnips.

variations

The basic cream of vegetable soup recipe can be varied using different vegetables, flavorings and seasonings as in the following:

Broccoli

Cut 1 kg broccoli into florets, finely chop thick stalks, season with ½ tsp nutmeg and reserve 1 tsp lemon juice to serve from the top along with 2 tbsp finely chopped broccoli florets.

Carrot and Orange

Add 1 kg diced carrots to the basic recipe. Just before liquidising add 2 cups of fresh orange juice and 1 tbsp sugar. Garnish with a slice of fresh orange and a whirl of whipped cream piped on top and sprinkled with freshly grated carrot.

Spinach and Potato

500 gms spinach leaves (approx. 6 bunches) cleaned, washed, boiled in hot water and 2-3 large potatoes grated. Add ½ tsp grated nutmeg. Add all this to the stock, liquidise and sieve. Garnish with toasted almonds and beaten fresh cream.

Asparagus and Basil

Add 1 kg Asparagus to the stock, liquidise and sieve. Garnish with ½ tsp chopped basil and sour cream.

Mushroom

Take 1 kg fresh mushrooms, including the stalks and cook for half an hour and add to the stock, liquidise and sieve. Garnish with 2 mushrooms that have been fried in butter and drained well on kitchen paper, along with a large sprig of parsley.

Almond

450 gms of almonds blanched, skinned and put in the blender with 3 cups of water and puréed. Strain through a sieve and add one extra cup of water and 250 gms of boiled potatoes and liquidise again and strain. Add this to the basic recipe and garnish with thinly sliced and slightly toasted almonds. Serve hot or cold.

Cauliflower Cheese

Take 1 kg cauliflower, ½ tsp sugar, ½ tsp nutmeg, and ½ tsp mustard. Cook gently for 45 minutes, add stock then liquidise and sieve. When re-heating, add 100 gms of cauliflower florets that have been lightly fried in oil and drained well. Sprinkle very finely grated cheese on each bowl as the soup is being served.

Soup in a Blanket

ingredients

250 gms	Puff pastry dough
1 tbsp	Butter
2 cups	White vegetable stock (leeks, celery, onion, pumpkin, herbs)
½ cup	Finely chopped carrots ⎫
½ cup	Finely chopped green beans ⎬ parboiled
½ cup	Small pieces asparagus tips ⎭
1 cup	Milk
1 tbsp	Olive oil

To Sprinkle
Finely chopped fresh basil and Parmesan cheese.

*You will need 4 individual ceramic dishes to serve.

method

Heat oil in a heavy saucepan over medium heat and add the carrots, green beans and asparagus. Sauté until the vegetables are soft. Add the stock and simmer it for 5-7 minutes. Add milk and season with salt and pepper. Divide the soup into 4 ceramic soup bowls, sprinkle with Parmesan and basil and keep aside. 20 minutes before you want to serve roll out the puff pastry dough and cut to fit the size of the bowl. Press down the edges to seal. Make a design on the dough to look like a blanket and bake it in the oven for 15 minutes or until light brown.

CORN CHOWDER

ingredients

2 tbsp	Butter
1	Medium sized onion, finely chopped
½ each	Green and red pepper, finely chopped
1 tbsp	Whole wheat flour
2	Medium sized potatoes, parboiled and finely chopped
450 gms	Canned or fresh boiled yellow corn
1¼ cups	Milk
1 cup	Light vegetable stock (made with onion, celery, turnip, white pumpkin, mushroom stalks, parsley, thyme)
1 tsp	Salt
½ tsp	Pepper
1 cup	Fresh cream, beaten
4 oz	Mushrooms, washed and sliced (optional)

To Serve
50 gms grated cheese

method

In a small frying pan, melt butter over moderate heat. Add onions and peppers. Cook, stirring occasionally, for 5-7 minutes. Remove the frying pan from the heat and stir in the flour. Set aside. Put the potatoes, corn, stock and milk into a large saucepan and place over moderate heat. Bring the mixture to a boil, stirring occasionally. Pour a little of the liquid into the pepper mixture. Stir to form a smooth thick liquid and stir this into the potato mixture. If using mushrooms, add them now. Cover the pan and simmer for 20 minutes. Season with salt, pepper and add the cream. Blend thoroughly. Heat for a few minutes over low heat and serve immediately.

Serves 4-6

Cheddar Wafers

ingredients

1 cup	Grated Cheddar cheese
2 tbsp	Butter, softened
¼ tsp	Garlic salt
½ tsp	Worcestershire sauce
¼ tsp	Dry mustard
¼ tsp	Tabasco
¼ tsp	Pepper
1 cup	Plain flour, sieved with ½ tsp baking powder
½ tsp	Dried herbs of your choice
½ tsp	Salt

method

In a mixing bowl beat together cheese, butter, Worcestershire sauce, mustard, Tabasco, garlic salt, pepper and herbs at medium speed until smooth. Then, lower the speed and add the flour. Gather the dough into a ball and knead it a few times on a lightly floured surface. Shape the dough into a 12" log, wrap it in plastic and refrigerate until firm. Preheat the oven to 350°F. Sprinkle the baking sheet with a little salt. Slice the log into ¼" thick slices and arrange the slices 1" apart on the baking sheet. Bake the wafers for about 20 minutes and cool them before serving.

Stuffed Snow Peas

ingredients

450 gms	Chinese pea pods (snow peas)
1	Tomato, finely chopped
1 tbsp	Finely chopped basil
1 cup	Sour cream
½ tsp	Ready mustard
	Salt and pepper to taste

method

In a medium saucepan, bring 3 cups of lightly salted water to a boil. Carefully lower trimmed pea pods into boiling water. Simmer over medium heat for about 1 minute until crisp but tender, then drain. Immediately immerse the pea pods in cold water. Drain again and refrigerate for at least 30 minutes until chilled. In a small bowl, combine tomato, basil, sour cream, mustard, salt and pepper. With a sharp knife, carefully slit one side of the pea pod. Use a small spoon and fill each pea pod with the sour cream mixture. Arrange the filled pods on a baking tray with raised sides. Arrange them so as to keep them upright. Refrigerate for 1 hour and serve cold as a starter

Serves 4-6

ALMOND DIP

ingredients

50 gms (¼ cup)	Blanched almonds
1 clove	Garlic, crushed
½ tsp	White pepper
1 tsp	Salt
2	Small tomatoes, skinned and finely chopped
3 tbsp	Red wine vinegar
½ cup	Olive oil

To Serve
Assorted raw vegetables

method

Toast the almonds in the oven at 350°F for 7-10 minutes until lightly browned. Put them in a liquidiser with garlic, salt, pepper, tomatoes and vinegar. Blend to a smooth paste. Now blend in the olive oil a little at a time, making sure each spoon is absorbed before adding any more. Beat it constantly, until the sauce is thick and creamy. Pour into a serving bowl and serve with crudités. Here are some suggestions for the fresh vegetables that you could use:

- Broccoli /cauliflower florets
- Carrots strips
- Celery strips
- Mushrooms quarters
- Courgette fingers

BREAD CANAPÉS

ingredients

For the Canapés

| 12 slices | White bread, thinly sliced with the crusts removed |
| | Butter for greasing |

*You will need a cup cake tin with 12 cups

For the Filling

½ cup	Cottage cheese, chopped into small pieces
¼ cup	Chopped cashewnuts
2 tbsp	Oil or butter
2	Medium sized onions, finely chopped
1 tsp	Cumin powder
1 tsp	Curry powder
½ tsp	Garam masala
1 tsp	Green chilli and ginger paste
6 cloves	Garlic, crushed
1 tbsp	Currants (optional)
½ cup	Boiled peas
2 tbsp	Yogurt
½ cup	Chopped coriander leaves
	Salt to taste

method

For the Canapés

Grease the cup cake tins with butter. Take the bread slices, wet them slightly on both sides and press them into the tin. Apply butter on top and crisp them in a hot oven (150°C) for about 20-25 minutes. Remove from the oven and cool on a rack.

For the Filling

Fry the pieces of cottage cheese and the cashews in hot oil or butter alternately and set aside. In the remaining oil fry the onions until light brown. Add cumin, garam masala, chilli-ginger paste, garlic, currants and sauté. Then add cottage cheese, cashews, salt, peas, yogurt, curry powder and coriander leaves. Cook until the mixture gets dry. Fill the canapés with the mixture just before serving and sprinkle the fresh coriander on top.

Makes 12 servings

Barbecued Corn on the Cob with Cheese Butter

ingredients

6	Corn on the cob with the husk
100 gms	Butter, softened
50 gms	Sharp Cheddar cheese, shredded
2 tbsp	Finely chopped spring onions
½ tsp	Worcestershire sauce
¼ tsp each	Pepper and chilli powder

method

Pull down a few husks and silk from the corn, rinse the corn and soak it for 15 minutes. Meanwhile, for the cheese butter, combine all the ingredients in a mixing bowl. Stir till blended and set aside. Remove corn from the water and cook directly over coal till tender, turning frequently. Remove husks and serve with cheese butter.

COTTAGE CHEESE MOULD

ingredients

1 cup	Cottage cheese
1 cup	Sour cream
1 tsp	Lemon juice
1 tsp	Worcestershire sauce
2 cloves	Garlic
½ tsp	Salt
2½ tsp	Gelatine
1	Vegetable stock cube
¼ cup	Chilled white wine
50 gms	Miniature tomatoes
3 stems	Green onions, finely chopped
3 slices	Lemon
¼ cup	Yellow corn OR chopped yellow pepper

To Serve
Thinly sliced toasted bread or crackers

method

In a blender combine cottage cheese, sour cream, garlic, lemon juice, Worcestershire Sauce and salt. Blend until smooth. In a small saucepan sprinkle the gelatine over the wine; Stir over low heat until the gelatine dissolves. Add a stock cube to it. Gradually stir the gelatine mixture into the cottage cheese mixture. Adjust the seasoning and pour into a 7" spring form pan. Refrigerate until firm (4 – 6 hours). Invert the firmly set mould onto a large round platter. Garnish with tomatoes, onions, lemon wedges and yellow corn. Serve with toasted bread or crackers.

Makes 35 appetizer servings

WELSH RAREBIT

ingredients

25 gms	Butter
25 gms	Plain flour
½ cup	Milk, cold
1 tsp	Ready mustard
1 tsp	Beer, ale or Worcestershire sauce
200 gms	Cheese, grated
4 slices	Buttered toast

To Garnish
Sprigs of parsley

method

Heat the butter in a saucepan. Stir in the flour and cook steadily for several minutes. Gradually add cold milk. Bring to a boil and cook until smooth and thick. Add the mustard, salt, pepper, beer and most of the cheese. Heat steadily without boiling until the cheese has melted. Spread this over the hot buttered toast. Sprinkle with the remainder of the cheese and brown under a hot grill. Garnish with parsley and serve at once.

ASPARAGUS ROLLS

ingredients

8 thick spears	Fresh or tinned asparagus
100 gms	Butter, softened
1 tbsp	Coarse grained mustard
8 thin slices	White bread
	Grated rind of 1 lemon
	Salt and pepper to taste

method

If using fresh asparagus, blanch in boiling salt water till just tender. If using tinned asparagus, drain all the water and place the spears on a plate to dry out. In a small bowl, blend $2/_3$ of the butter with the mustard, lemon rind and seasoning. Spread over the bread slices. Lay one asparagus spear on the edge of each bread slice and roll it up lightly. Place the rolls join side down on a lightly greased baking sheet. Melt the remaining butter and brush it over the rolls. Heat the oven to 375°F or 190°C and bake for 12-15 minutes until golden and crisp. Cool slightly before serving.

Serves 8

CRACKERS AND SPREADS

Here are a few spreads you can serve with savoury biscuits or small triangles of toast or bread.

SPECKLED TOMATO SPREAD

ingredients

2	Medium sized tomatoes, blanched, peeled, deseeded and chopped
1 cup	Cheddar cheese, finely grated
1½ tbsp (each)	Finely chopped parsley and chives

method

Combine all the ingredients in a mixing bowl, beating with a wooden spoon until they are well blended. Chill for 30 minutes before serving.

Makes 1 cup

CREAM CHEESE AND HERB SPREAD

ingredients

4 oz (100 gms)	Cream cheese
1 tbsp	Mayonnaise
1 tsp each	finely chopped parsley and chives
	Salt and pepper to taste

method

Combine all the ingredients in a medium size mixing bowl, beating with a wooden spoon until well blended. Chill for 30 minutes and serve.

Makes ½ cup

CURRY SPREAD

ingredients

1 box (225 gms)	Cream cheese spread
¼ cup	Sour cream
2 tsp	Curry powder
¼ tsp	Garlic salt
½ cup	Finely chopped peanuts
1	Tomato, finely chopped (remove the liquid)
2 tbsp	Finely chopped green onions
1 tbsp	Finely chopped basil

To Serve
Crisp toast or sesame crackers

method

In a medium sized bowl, combine cream cheese, sour cream, curry powder and garlic salt. Stir until smooth. Stir in the peanuts, tomato and basil. Spoon into a serving bowl, sprinkle the onions evenly over it. Serve with toast or crackers.

Makes 2 cups

CHEESE AND HERB PÂTÉ WITH MELBA TOAST

ingredients

150 gms	Butter, melted
450 gms	Cream cheese
3 cloves	Garlic, freshly crushed with a little salt
3 tbsp	Freshly chopped parsley, chives, marjoram

To Serve
15 pieces Melba toast

method

In a bowl beat cream cheese with the crushed garlic and the fresh herbs, and then gently fold the cooled melted butter into the mixture. Do not add the butter while hot or the mixture will curdle. Transfer the paté to a tin of your choice and press it down. (For this recipe you'll need a 1 lb loaf tin). Chill for about an hour or till ready to serve. When you want to serve, unmould it onto a serving plate decorated with lettuce leaves and sliced tomatoes. Serve with crisp Melba toast on the side.

Options

1) Press paté into a piping bag and pipe stars over small tart cases and decorate with a piece of walnut and chopped celery.
2) Pipe paté into a scooped tomato or pepper, chill and slice. Serve as a surrounding to a tossed salad.
3) Peel, cut in half and remove the seeds from a cucumber. Pipe in the paté and garnish with black olives and chopped walnuts. Serve chilled.

BURGER BITES

ingredients

12	Small size buns, halved
1 tbsp	Olive oil
2 cups	Mashed potatoes
1 cup	Finely chopped mixed boiled vegetables
1	Onion, finely chopped
2 cloves	Garlic, chopped
¼ tsp	Dried oregano, crushed
2 tbsp	Tomato ketchup
150 gms or 3 slices	Mozzarella cheese
2 tbsp	Butter
	Bread crumbs to coat
	Salt and pepper to taste

To Serve
Prepared mustard and tomato ketchup

To Garnish
Potato sticks

method

Butter the bun halves lightly and toast them in the oven until crisp. Sauté the onions in olive oil, add oregano, potatoes, mixed vegetables, salt and pepper. Mix well and add ketchup. Take this mixture off the stove and let it cool. Form the mixture into small patties (the same size as the bun) and roll the patties in the breadcrumbs. Cut the mozzarella into small triangles (again the same size as the bun). Now place the patties on the buns and cover with the cheese triangles. Bake in a preheated oven at 350°F for 10-15 minutes until the cheese melts. Arrange them on a platter surrounded by potato sticks and serve hot with mustard and ketchup.

Makes 24 appetizer servings

TRADITIONAL COLESLAW

ingredients

450 gms	Shredded white cabbage
2	Carrots, grated
2 sticks	Celery, trimmed
1	Small green pepper, sliced long
1 tbsp	Finely chopped onion
5-6 tbsp	Mayonnaise
1 level tsp	Sugar
½ tsp (each)	Salt and pepper
½ tsp	Lemon juice

method

Mix together mayonnaise, sugar, salt, pepper, lemon juice and finely chopped onion. Cut the vegetables as explained above. Put them in a large salad bowl, and chill. Just before serving, add dressing and toss well.

VEGETABLE JALOUSIE
Puff Pastry Pie

ingredients

5 cups	Mixed boiled vegetables such as babycorn, carrots, potatoes, peas, brussel sprouts etc. (cut into bite-sized pieces)
2½ cups	Paprika sauce (recipe follows)
250 gms	Puff pastry dough
½ cup	Grated sharp Cheddar cheese
2 tbsp	Butter
2	Onions, finely chopped
1	Green or red pepper, finely chopped
1 clove	Garlic, crushed
2 tbsp	Parsley, chopped
3 tbsp	Almond flakes

method

In a saucepan, melt 1 tbsp butter, sauté the onions, peppers, garlic and parsley for 3-4 minutes. Add the paprika sauce and mix thoroughly till all the vegetables are coated properly. Grease an 8" x 9" rectangular or an 8" diametre round baking dish. Pour the mixture in and sprinkle cheese and almonds and set aside. Roll out the pastry dough, ¼ inch thick or to suit the size of the dish. Carefully lift up the pastry, place it on top of the vegetables and lightly cut the pastry, as if making lines on it, to allow heat to pass through. Grease the top with the remaining butter and bake it in a hot oven at 150ºC for 15 - 30 minutes or until the crust is crisp and golden. Remove from the oven and serve right away.

PAPRIKA SAUCE

Melt 3 tbsp butter and add 2½ tbsp plain flour. Cool for 3-4 minutes. Add 2½ cups milk, stirring continuously. Season with salt and paprika. Bring to a boil and set aside.
Makes 2½ cups

Serves 4-6

GREEN GODDESS DIP

ingredients

200 gms	Cream cheese spread
1 cup	Sour cream (½ thick curd, ½ fresh cream mixed with 1 tbsp lemon juice and 1 tsp salt)
2 cloves	Garlic, minced
¼ cup	Finely chopped green onions
¼ cup	Minced parsley
½ tsp	Dried tarragon leaves
¼ tsp	Pepper
1 tbsp	Vinegar

To Serve
Fresh raw vegetables and corn chips

method

In a blender jar mix together cream cheese, garlic, green onions, parsley, tarragon leaves, pepper, vinegar, and blend until mixed. Pour it out into a bowl and fold in sour cream. Chill until ready to serve. Serve with fresh raw vegetables or corn chips as dippers.

Makes 1½ cups

TRADITIONAL WAFFLES

ingredients

4	Eggs
2 cups	Plain flour, sifted*
1 tsp	Salt
1 tsp	Baking soda
1 tsp	Baking powder
2 cups	Buttermilk
1 cup	Melted butter

To Serve
Hot maple syrup or golden syrup

*Sift the flour before measuring

method

Beat the eggs until light. Sift together flour, salt, soda and baking soda. Add the flour mixture and buttermilk alternately to the beaten eggs, beginning and ending with the flour mixture. Add melted butter; blend thoroughly. Store in the fridge until used. Remove from the fridge ½ an hour before you want to use it. Heat the waffle iron 10 minutes prior to use. For each waffle, pour about ½ cup batter into the centre of the lower half of the waffle iron until it spreads 1 inch from the edges. Shut the cover gently and cook until the iron stops steaming. Do not raise the cover during baking. Remove and serve immediately with butter and hot maple syrup.

Makes 8 Waffles

This recipe is also used for different types of flavors. Some of the options I really liked are as follows...

1. When you want sweet waffles, simply add 1 tbsp powdered sugar to the batter and serve with the desired flavouring.

   a) Heat ½ cup of maple syrup and additional melted butter to serve.
   b) Heat ½ cup strawberry purée along with ½ cup sugar, 2 tsp cornstarch and 1 tsp lemon juice. Bring to a boil until slightly thickened and translucent. Serve warm.
   c) Mix 1 tsp powdered cinnamon with ½ cup of powdered sugar and sprinkle this onto hot waffles.

2. When you want savory waffles. Do not add sugar, simply follow the above basic recipe and vary the flavouring as desired.

   a) Take 2 cups of waffle batter in a bowl, add 2-3 tbsp of grated cheese mixed with ½ tsp of mustard, ½ tsp black pepper, 2 tbsp Each, finely chopped onions and tomato. Mix thoroughly and pour into the hot waffle iron. Bake for 8-10 minutes and serve with sour cream flavored with chives.
   b) To make herb waffles, take 2 cups of waffle batter simply add 2 tbsp of chopped fresh herbs of your choice. Serve this with creamy mashed potatoes to which you have added cream cheese.
   c) If you want a Mexican flavor to your waffles, reduce plain flour by 1 cup and add 1 cup of maize flour and proceed as per recipe. You could serve these waffles with spicy red salsa, Refried beans, Monterey Jack cheese and sour cream.

Eggless Waffles

ingredients

2 cups	Plain flour
½ tsp	Salt
1 tsp	Sugar
2 tsp	Baking powder
1½ tsp	Soda bicarbonate
2 cups	Thick buttermilk
6 tbsp	Melted butter

To Serve
Hot maple syrup or golden syrup

method

Sieve the flour with salt, baking powder, soda and sugar. Mix buttermilk with the butter. Mix wet and dry ingredients alternately little at a time, to make a smooth batter. Cover and keep for ½ an hour. Heat the waffle iron 10 minutes prior to serving. Apply a little butter on the iron and pour the mixture with a ladle to cover the iron plates. Bake for 8-10 minutes or until light brown. Remove and serve immediately with hot syrup.

Note For variations, refer to Traditional Waffle recipe.

Makes 8 Waffles

VEGETABLE SIZZLERS

ingredients

100 gms	Spaghetti (boiled in salted water)
½ cup	White sauce (made from ½ tsp butter, ½ tsp flour, ½ cup milk)
2 tbsp	Grated cheese
100 gms	French beans (cut long and boiled)
100 gms	Carrots (cut long and boiled)
100 gms	Green peas (shelled)
100 gms	Onions (sliced)
3	Potatoes (cut into thin strips and fried)
200 gms	Cottage cheese (cut into 1" cubes)
2	Corn on the cob (cut into 2" pieces and boiled)
100 gms	Capsicum (cut into cubes)
3	Ripe tomatoes (cut lengthwise into 6)
2 cups	Cooked rice mixed with ½ cup tomato purée salt and pepper
	Olive oil for sautéing

For the Tomato and Herb Sauce

½ kg	Ripe tomatoes (chopped)
1	Onion (chopped)
1 clove	Garlic, crushed
1	Carrot (grated)
2 tbsp	Oil
1 tsp	Sugar
¼ cup	Vegetable stock
3 tsp	Worcestershire sauce
½ tsp	Basil (dried)
½ tsp	Oregano (dried)

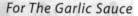

For The Garlic Sauce

10-12 cloves	Garlic, finely chopped
2 tbsp	Chopped coriander
1 tbsp	Olive oil
1 cup	Vegetable stock
2 tbsp	Corn flour
	Salt and pepper to taste

For the Sizzling Sauce

½ cup	Water
2 tbsp	Soya sauce
1 tbsp	Worcestershire sauce
2 tbsp	Butter

*You will need 2 sizzler plates to serve

method

Mix the spaghetti with the white sauce and cheese. Season with salt and pepper and set aside. Then sauté the mixed boiled vegetables in olive oil. Season with salt and set aside. Sauté the pieces of cottage cheese carefully on both sides in oil. Season with salt and set aside.

Apply a little butter on each side of the pieces of corn. Season with salt and set aside. Sauté the onions, tomatoes and capsicum separately in olive oil. Season with salt and set aside. At this point, place the iron sizzler plates in the oven to heat.

For the Tomato and Herb Sauce

Heat oil in a vessel, fry the onions, garlic and carrots for 5 minutes. Add the finely chopped skinned tomatoes, vegetable stock, Worcestershire sauce and herbs. Boil the mixture for 20 minutes. Purée the mixture in a blender and then return it to the pan. Simmer for 15 minutes more and set aside.

Makes 1½ cups

For the Garlic Sauce
Heat oil in a saucepan and fry the garlic in it for 4-5 minutes. Mix corn flour in the vegetable stock and add it to the garlic along with coriander, salt and pepper. Boil until thick (about 10-15 minutes).

Makes 1¼ cups

For the Sizzling Sauce
Mix water, Soya sauce and, Worcestershire sauce, and set the mixture to boil. Set butter aside for sizzling.

how to proceed

Keep the heated sizzler plates on the gas and lightly grease them with oil. Arrange the spaghetti on the outer rim of the plate. Then arrange the vegetables, potato chips, onions, capsicum and tomato. Then the cottage cheese and corn arranged alternately with the rice. Just before serving, boil the sizzling sauce and pour it over your sizzler at the table, with butter to make the sizzling sound with the 2 sauces served at the side. Garlic bread is a good accompaniment to the sizzler.

Note To make a sizzling sound the plate as well as the sauces should be very hot.

SHEPHERD'S PIE

ingredients

For the Vegetable Stew

3 cups	Mixed vegetables, cut into ½ " cubes (florets of cauliflower and broccoli, carrots, mushrooms, peas, onions, zucchini, asparagus etc.)
2 cloves	Garlic, finely chopped
3 tbsp	Butter
1 cup	Vegetable stock
2 tbsp	Olive oil
1 tbsp each	Finely chopped parsley and thyme
	Salt and pepper to taste

For the Sauce

2 tbsp	Butter
1 tbsp	Olive oil
½ tsp	Salt
1	Onion, chopped
1 tbsp	Worcestershire sauce
1	Bay leaf
1 tsp	Tabasco
1 tsp	Thyme
1 tsp	Tarragon
3 cloves	Garlic, chopped
½ cup	Red wine
3 tbsp	Plain flour
3 cups	Stock made with mushrooms, carrots, celery, onions, leeks, parsley and garlic
2 tbsp	Finely chopped parsley

For the Potato Blanket

4	Medium sized potatoes
3 tbsp	Butter
½ cup	Fresh cream
	Salt and pepper to taste

method

For the Stew

Wash and dry all the vegetables. Bring a pot of water to the boil. Add salt and parboil all the vegetables separately and rinse them. Heat the butter and olive oil in a large casserole dish. Add the onions and carrots and cook for 3-4 minutes. Add salt and a little water. Cook until soft. Add the rest of the vegetables along with the garlic and herbs and the additional water/stock. Cook for 15-20 minutes until all the vegetables are tender and set aside.

For the Sauce

Heat the butter and oil in a saucepan. Add onions, thyme, the bay leaf and salt. Cook over low heat until the onions are nicely browned. Stir in the garlic and wine and reduce by half. Add the flour. Cook for 2 minutes and simmer the sauce with the stock for approx. 20 minutes. Add the parsley and check the seasoning. Add this to the stew.

For the Potato Blanket

Boil and mash the potatoes until smooth. Mix butter, cream, salt and pepper. Fill this into a pastry bag with a large nozzle.

to assemble

Preheat the oven to 350°F. Grease a casserole dish with butter and ladle the stew into the dish. Smoothen the surface and pipe the potato mixture over the surface like a blanket. Bake until the potatoes are slightly browned and the sauce bubbles to the surface. Serve hot.

Note Slightly warmed French bread with cheese goes very well with this.

SANDWICH LOAF

ingredients

1	Large sandwich loaf (white or brown)
200 gms	Butter
250 gms	Cottage cheese
3 cups	Mayonnaise
100 gms	Whipped cream
	Salt, pepper and mustard to taste

various layers to choose from

- 1 tin — Baked beans, sautéed with finely chopped onions and capsicum
- 1 packet — Cheese slices
- 250 gms — Yellow corn, boiled and sautéed with peppers
- 1 cup — Egg mayonnaise (optional)
- 4 large — Potatoes, boiled and sliced
- 4-5 — Medium sized onions, sliced
- ½ cup — Sliced olives
- 6 — Large firm tomatoes, sliced
- 1 cup — Russian salad (mixed with boiled vegetables, finely chopped and tossed with mayonnaise and seasoned)
- 1 tin — Green asparagus tips
- 3-4 slices — Cheese

To Garnish
A few sprigs of parsley
Grated carrots
Thinly sliced red, yellow and green peppers
1 large head of lettuce

method

Slice the crusts off the loaf and cut the loaf lenghtwise into 6-8 slices. Cream the butter until light, add salt, pepper and mustard to taste. Butter each slice and place them in a damp cloth. Place 2 cups of mayonnaise in a blender, add the grated cottage cheese and blend well. Turn this out in a bowl and fold in the cream. Season to taste and chill. Choose 6 different layers from the above variations. Prepare them and set aside.

to assemble

Place one slice of bread on a serving dish, spread a thin layer of mayonnaise (from remaining 1 cup) on it and then spread one of the layers evenly. Place another slice of bread on top of it and proceed the same way with the various fillings. Layer all the slices in the same way and finish it off with the topmost slice of the loaf. Now spread or pipe creamy mayonnaise onto the top and sides. garnish attractively with lettuce leaves, grated carrot, olive slices, finely chopped parsley, and thinly sliced red, yellow and green peppers. Chill thoroughly. Approx. 4-6 hours. Serve, cutting slices vertically.

ENGLISH HIGH TEA

In the olden days, afternoon tea or high tea played an important role in the lives of the people in northern England. There were tea cakes, scones, gingerbread, cucumber sandwiches, short bread, cookies, tarts and so on... Inclusive of all this, afternoon tea was stylishly served with a fresh tablecloth, wooden trays, beautiful china and tea made the old fashioned way.

METHOD FOR TRADITIONAL TEA

Warm the tea pot first with a little boiling water (china is better than silver or steel) and then, after putting in the tea (one heaped teaspoon per person), put in water which is still boiling (use cold water for boiling as it has more dissolved oxygen which gives a better flavour to the tea). As the gush of boiling water hits the tea leaves, the leaves unfurl quickly to give out their delicate flavour. Let it rest in the teapot for 5-7 minutes and then pour it out in a cup through a strainer and serve with a slice of lime and sugar, or milk and sugar.

To make mint tea, throw in 8-10 large sprigs of fresh mint, coarsely chopped into one pint of boiling water. Infuse for 3 minutes and then strain.

There are various types of teas available. They range from English breakfast to Darjeeling, Earl Grey, fruit flavors, mint, green tea, lemon grass, rose petal etc. On a hot summer afternoon you could also enjoy mild tea served in a tall glass liberally filled with ice, fresh mint, sugar, lemon juice and a few rose petals to give a pleasant, cooling feeling.

Now, let us look at some of the goodies to go with the tea...

Opposite (clockwise)
i) Goat's Cheese and Sundried Tomato Tartlets ii) English Tea
iii) Ginger Bread iv) Cucumber Sandwiches
v) Scones with Fresh Strawberry Jam and Clotted Cream

Scones

ingredients

450 gms	Self-raising flour
175 gms	Butter, softened
3 tbsp	Castor sugar, sieved
2	Eggs, lightly beaten OR
4 tbsp	Condensed milk (for eggless version)
½ cup	Milk
	A pinch of salt
	Currants, to taste

method

Preheat the oven to 220ºC or 425ºF. Sieve the flour with salt in a large bowl. Rub in the butter very gently until the mixture resembles crumbs. Add sugar, currants and beaten eggs and milk mixture. Be careful not to make the dough too soft or too dry. Turn it out onto a lightly floured board and cut into diamond shaped pieces or cut it with a two inch round cookie cutter (do not roll the mixture out and then cut into circles). Put onto trays and bake for approximately 25 minutes. Serve hot with clotted cream and strawberry jam.

Note Savoury scones can be made the same way by using grated cheese and crushed coriander instead of sugar and currants.

Opposite (clockwise)
i) Soup in a Blanket ii) Cheese and Herb Pãté with Melba Toast *Makes 14-16 pieces* **173**
iii) Barbecued Corn on the Cob with Cheese Butter

CLOTTED CREAM

ingredients

1 cup	Fresh cream at room temperature
$^1/_3$ cup	Sour cream at room temperature
1 tbsp	Icing sugar

method

An hour before serving, pour the cream into a bowl and whip until soft peaks form. Whisk in the sour cream and sugar and continue to beat until the mixture is very thick. Put it in the fridge and chill until ready to serve. It will stay fresh for about 4-6 hours.

Makes 1½ cups

HOME MADE STRAWBERRY JAM

ingredients

450 gms	Small strawberries
400 gms	Whole sugar
1 tsp	Lemon juice

method

Simply put washed strawberries into a pan and start cooking. Add sugar and stir from time to time until it forms a thick syrup. Take it off the heat and add the lemon juice. Leave it to cool and then pour into a jar and seal.

Makes 2 cups

Ginger Bread

ingredients

6 oz Or 175 gms	Self-raising flour
½ tsp	Mixed spices, cinnamon cloves and nutmeg
2 oz Or 50 gms	Brown sugar
2 tsp	Ground, fresh ginger
2 oz Or 50 gms	Butter
2 tbsp	Golden syrup or molasses
2	Eggs OR
4 tbsp	Condensed milk
¼ pint OR 150 ml	Milk
1 tsp	Baking soda
2 tbsp	Powdered sugar

method

Place all the ingredients in a large mixing bowl except for the milk and baking soda. Mix vigorously and then pour in the milk that has just been brought below boiling point. Add the soda and blend until nice and bubbly. It will look like pancake batter, which you pour into a non-stick 1 lb tin and bake at 180ºC for an hour. Remove from tin and cool on a wire rack and sprinkle with powdered sugar and slice as required.

CUCUMBER SANDWICHES

ingredients

1	Small cucumber, peeled and thinly sliced
1 tbsp	Wine vinegar
6 thin slices	White bread
	Unsalted butter
	Salt and pepper to taste

method

Combine the cucumber and wine vinegar in a bowl and toss to blend. Let it stand for ½ an hour. Drain off the excess liquid. Spread a thin coating of butter on each slice of bread. On 3 slices place the cucumber slices, making sure that the bread is well covered. Season with salt and pepper. Cover up with the remaining slices of bread. Trim the crusts and cut the sandwiches into 4.

Makes 12 square pieces

Sundried Tomato and Cheese Tartlets

ingredients

8	Small tartlet cases
2 tbsp	Thick cream
¼ cup	Goat cheese or cottage cheese, crumbled
2 tbsp	Minced, sun dried tomatoes
2	Sun dried tomatoes, sliced
	Freshly chopped herbs
	Red chilli pepper and salt to taste

method

Combine cheese and cream until smooth. Add the minced tomatoes, garlic, herbs and chilli, mixing thoroughly. This spread can be kept in the fridge for 3 days. To assemble the tartlets, fill each shell with the spread and top with a thin slice of the sun dried tomato. Serve at room temperature or heat it in the toaster oven for 5 minutes.

APPLE CRESCENTS

ingredients

250 gms	Puff pastry dough
300 gms	Cooking apples, peeled and finely diced
2 tbsp	Castor sugar
½ tsp	Cinnamon powder
	A few seedless raisins (optional)

To Serve
Sweetened whipped cream

method

Roll out the pastry dough on a floured surface to ¼ inch thickness. Cut out as many 4-inch rounds as possible. This will give you approximately 10 rounds. Dampen the edges with water and fold to make half moons. Enclose the apple in this and seal the edges. Brush lightly with water and sprinkle with sugar. Place on baking sheets and bake in a preheated oven for 220°C for 15 minutes or until golden. Transfer to a wire rack to cool. Carefully split the crescents along the joint and pipe in the whipped cream. Alternatively you could make these savoury by filling with spinach and cheese or mushroom and cheese.

Makes 8-10

BLUEBERRY MUFFINS

ingredients

2 cups	Plain flour, sifted
1½ tsp	Baking powder
¼ tsp	Salt
½ cup	Butter, softened
1 cup	Castor sugar
2	Eggs, beaten
1 tsp	Vanilla essence
½ cup	Milk
½ cup	Blueberries, dried

method

Pre heat the oven to 375°F. Either use 18 paper cups or greased muffin pan cups. Sift plain flour with baking powder and salt. Set aside. In a large bowl, beat the butter, sugar, eggs and vanilla until light and fluffy (about 4 minutes). Now lower the speed and beat in the flour alternately with milk and beat until smooth. With a rubber spatula, fold in the blueberries just until combined. Scoop about ¼ cup of the batter into each cup until $^2/_3$ full. Bake for about 20-25 minutes or until golden brown. Remove from the oven and cool. Sprinkle sugar on top.

Note You could replace blueberries with cranberries or black current for a change.

TOMATO MOULD

ingredients

2 cups	Tomato juice
2 tbsp	Olive oil
2	Onions, finely chopped
2 cloves	Garlic, finely chopped
1	Bay leaf
1 tsp	Lemon juice
2 tsp	Gelatine soaked in 2 tbsp vegetable stock
100 gms	Fresh cream
2 tbsp	Cream cheese
1 tsp	Sugar
	A dash of Tabasco
	Salt and Pepper to taste

To Garnish
Small bunches of parsley

To Serve
Whole wheat toast, thinly sliced

method

Heat the oil. Cook the onion and garlic. Add tomato juice, bay leaf, salt and pepper. Cook for 5 minutes. Slowly pour the gelatine mixture into the boiling tomato juice, stirring constantly. Add lemon juice and let it cool to room temperature. Remove the bay leaf and liquidise the mixture. Add cream cheese and fresh cream. Pour this into a 1½ pint oiled mould and freeze for 3 hours or overnight. Turn this out on a serving plate, garnish with small bunches of parsley and serve with crisp wholewheat toast.

Serves 4-6

The French have a way with food. In this cuisine, one can create many spectacular dishes using the same ingredients. Even for vegetarians there are aromatic herbs that blend with various dairy products to produce deliciously rich dishes. And not to forget the most delectable desserts created by French patisserie chefs. Here are some of the most popular recipes, authentically documented, to bring you the pleasure and satisfaction of continental cooking.

French Cuisine

BROCCOLI AND BOURSIN SOUP

ingredients

500 gms	Broccoli florets, chopped
1	Large onion, chopped
1	Large carrot, chopped
1	Large zucchini, chopped
1	Medium sized potato, chopped
1	2" piece of white pumpkin, chopped
1 stem	Celery
1 clove	Garlic
8 cups	Stock/Water
2 tbsp	Butter
2	Sunflower oil
75 gms	Boursin Cheese
	Salt and pepper to taste

To Garnish
Almond flakes
Whipped cream

method

Put all the vegetables into a large saucepan together with the butter, oil and 3 tbsp of stock/water. Heat the ingredients until they start to sizzle and then stir well. Cover and cook gently for 15 minutes shaking the pan occasionally, until all the vegetables are soft. Add the rest of the stock/water, season with salt and pepper and bring to a boil. Cover and simmer gently for 25 minutes. Strain the vegetables, liquidise and strain and then return them to the pan with the reserved liquid. Bring the soup back to a gentle boil and stir in the cheese until it melts. Garnish with almond flakes and whipped cream.

Note Serve with crusty whole wheat bread

Opposite (clockwise)
i) Broccoli Boursin Soup ii) Crêpe Gruyère
iii) Mushroom Croustade

CRÉME VICHYSSOISE

ingredients

1 litre	White vegetable stock (¼ kg onions, ¼ kg potatoes, 4 tbsp chopped celery, 100 gms carrots, 100 gms turnips, 2 bay leaves, 900 ml of water, 2 tsp olive oil)
2 tbsp	Butter
4	Large leeks, sliced (only the white portion)
2	Medium sized potatoes, peeled and sliced
1 tsp	Salt
1	Onion, finely chopped
1 cup (200gms)	Single cream

To Garnish
Finely chopped chives
Whipped cream

method

In a large saucepan melt the butter over moderate heat. When the foam subsides, add onions and leeks. Fry for 8-10 minutes or until they are a light golden brown. Add the potatoes and vegetable stock and salt. Bring to a boil. Reduce the heat to low and simmer for 15 minutes or until the potatoes are tender. Remove the pan from the heat, purée in a blender and strain. Now add the cream, adjust the salt and allow it to cool to room temperature and then place it in the refrigerator to chill. Serve with chopped chives and swirl cream on the top. If you wish to serve the soup hot, return it to the stove after adding the cream and heat gently on a low flame for 5 minutes.

Opposite (clockwise)
Savoury Quiche

MOULIN ROUGE

Avocado Mousse Bouchées

ingredients

4	Ripe avocado pears + juice of 1 lemon
1 tsp each	Salt and pepper
½ cup	Mayonnaise
½ cup	Thick yogurt
¼ cup	Fresh cream, beaten
1 clove	Garlic
1 level tsp	Gelatine mixed with ½ cup of white wine or vegetable stock
12-15	Bouchées cases, made crisp in the oven

To Garnish
2 tbsp chives or parsley

method

Peel and chop the avocado, dribble lemon juice over it and combine with salt in an electric hand mixer along with garlic and mayonnaise. Blend together to form a smooth paste. Turn it out into a bowl and fold in the cream and yogurt. Gently heat the gelatine mixture until translucent, cool slightly and fold it into the avocado mixture. Cool it over a bowl of ice. When it is about to set, force it into a piping bag and pipe into crisp bouchée cases. Garnish with your choice of herbs. Alternatively you could pipe this mixture into tart cases and have avocado mousse tartlets.

Serves 8

MUSHROOM CROUSTADE

ingredients

4	Medium, short crust pastry tart cases OR
8	Small, short crust pastry tart cases
250 gms	Mushrooms, washed and cut into thin slices
50 gms	Butter
50 gms	Plain or whole wheat flour
½ litre	Cold milk
2 tbsp	Oil
150 gms	Gruyère cheese, grated
	Salt pepper and mustard to taste

method

Prepare the sauce. Melt butter in a saucepan, add flour and stir. Pour in cold milk all at one go and stir. Cook for 10 minutes at low heat stirring occasionally with a wooden spoon. Fry the sliced mushrooms with a pinch of salt in oil over low heat. When mushrooms are soft, remove them from heat and set aside. Pre-heat the oven to 425ºF or 220ºC. Add half the cheese to the sauce and stir. Pour a little of this sauce into each tart case. Divide the mushrooms equally between all the tart cases and put them on top of the sauce. Sprinkle the rest of the cheese on them and bake for 5 minutes. Serve hot.

LAYERED FRENCH LOAF

ingredients

1 loaf	French bread 20" x 2" (approx.)
1 cup	Grated sharp cheese
1 cup	Finely chopped tomato
2 tbsp	Chopped fresh basil
½ tsp	Finely chopped garlic
1 tbsp	Olive oil
¼ cup	Mayonnaise
¼ cup	Chopped olives
	Salt and pepper to taste

method

In a small bowl, combine olive and cheese and season with salt and pepper, set aside. In another bowl, combine the well drained tomatoes, basil, garlic, olive oil and again season with salt and pepper, set aside. Preheat the oven to 375⁰F. Cut the bread lengthwise into three equal slices. Spread the olive and cheese mixture evenly on the cut side of the bottom slice. Spread half the mayonnaise over it. Now, place the middle slice over this and spread the tomato mixture on this slice. Cover it with mayonnaise and top with the remaining bread slice. With the crusty side up, wrap the loaf in foil and bake for 15 minutes in the oven, until hot. Cut diagonally into 1" slices. Serve warm.

Makes about 20 slices

Salad Niçoise

ingredients

1 big head	Iceberg lettuce, cut into square pieces
2	Large capsicums, cut into 1" long strips
4-5	Spring onions, finely chopped
2	Medium sized firm tomatoes, cut into ½" cubes
3-4	Spinach leaves, cut into square pieces
5-6	Mushrooms, sliced vertically
2-3	Carrots, cut into small pieces
50 gms	Walnuts, chopped
4 sticks	Celery, trimmed and chopped
1 recipe	French dressing (recipe follows)

method

Wash and cut all the vegetables as explained above and chill them separately. When you want to serve the salad, put the prepared lettuce and spinach at the bottom of a large bowl and pile in all the other vegetables and top with the walnuts. I'd prefer to use a wooden bowl that is rubbed with a cut clove of garlic. I like to serve the dressing separately at the table and each one can take as much as they like.

Serves 4

FRENCH DRESSING

Mix together in a liquidiser, 2 cups oil (salad oil or olive oil), ½ cup wine vinegar, 2 tsp soft brown sugar, a pinch of salt, 2 level tsp dry mustard powder and the juice of ½ a lemon. Switch the liquidiser on for a few seconds until everything is perfectly combined. Transfer this to a decorative bottle or a sauce boat.

Makes 2½ cups

Salad Bowl With Walnut
And Dijon Mustard Dressing

ingredients

1 head	Iceberg lettuce, torn into bite-size pieces, washed with ice water and drained
1 head	Romaine lettuce
1 cup	Finely sliced green onions
½ cup	Spoon tomatoes, washed
½ cup	Fresh spinach leaves, torn into bite-size pieces
¼ cup	Walnuts, coarsely chopped and toasted
½ cup	Mayonnaise
1 tbsp	Lemon juice
1 tbsp	Olive oil
2 tsp	Grainy mustard
	Salt and pepper to taste

method

Prepare all the vegetables in a large salad bowl and chill until ready to use. In a small bowl, mix the mayonnaise, lemon juice, olive oil, mustard, salt and pepper. Just before serving, place the dressing at the bottom of the bowl and fill in all the vegetables. Scooping the vegetables from down to up, gently toss the salad. When all the vegetables are coated with the dressing, sprinkle the walnuts on top and serve right away.

Serves 4-6

MOULIN ROUGE

Ratatouille

ingredients

3	Medium sized aubergines, sliced
3	Medium sized courgettes, sliced
2	Medium sized onions, peeled and sliced
1	Green pepper, sliced
1	Red pepper, sliced
1 kg	Tomatoes, peeled and chopped
5 tbsp	Olive oil
4 cloves	Garlic, halved
1 tsp	Fresh thyme or oregano
2	Bay leaves
	Salt and freshly ground pepper to taste

method

In a heavy frying pan heat 2 tbsp olive oil and fry the onions and garlic. Cook until soft and remove from the frying pan. Add a little oil again and fry the aubergine until soft, remove from the pan and add salt and pepper to it. Set aside. In the same pan, fry the courgette, add a little water if it sticks to the pan. When half cooked, add sliced peppers and cook until the vegetables are soft. Now add the aubergine, onion and garlic that were set aside earlier. Mix well. Stir in the tomatoes along with salt, herbs and bay leaves. Cook for 10 minutes. Serve hot or cold.

MOULIN ROUGE

SAVOURY QUICHE

ingredients

For the Pastry

225 gms	Plain flour
125 gms	Plain butter, softened
1	Egg at room temperature
	A pinch of salt

For the Basic Cheese Custard

2	Eggs
1	Egg yolk
½ cup	Cheddar cheese
¼ cup	Gouda cheese
100 gms	Fresh cream
1 cup	Full fat milk
1 tbsp	Plain flour
	Salt, pepper, mustard and nutmeg for seasoning

variations for fillings

Onion 250 gms chopped onions lightly sautéed in 1 oz (2 tbsp) butter. Add 1 tbsp olive oil, then drain onto kitchen paper.

Mushrooms 1 packet of mushrooms sliced and sautéed in 1 oz of butter and 1 tbsp of olive oil. Then drained onto kitchen paper.

Red and Yellow Peppers 2 peppers cut into long strips and sautéed in 2 tbsp of olive oil. Then drain onto kitchen paper.

Asparagus 8 spears of tinned asparagus cut into pieces of 1 inch each, or 12 spears of fresh asparagus, steamed in salted water and cut into pieces of 1 inch each.

Tomato 3 medium sized tomatoes skinned and diced.

Spinach 1 bunch of fresh spinach, washed, boiled and finely chopped or mashed.

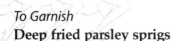

To Garnish
Deep fried parsley sprigs

method

For the Pastry
Sieve the flour with salt. Make a well in the centre, put the butter in it and break an egg over this. Using your fingertips, pat the egg into the butter. Now scoop the flour up from left to right, right to left and from the top to the bottom. You will slowly see the mixture forming large crumbs, at this point you may need to add 2 spoons of ice cold water to form a soft dough. If you are not using egg, follow the same procedure but, add a little more ice cold water while making the dough. It would be a good idea to freeze the dough for at least 2-3 hours or over night, if you wish. When you are ready to make the quiche, bring the dough out of the freezer, and let it thaw to room temperature. Roll it lightly into a 10" round and press it into 9.5" flan case. If you are making individual quiches, roll 8 rounds of 3.5" and press them into 3" individual pans. Prick the pastry all over with a fork and bake for 30-35 minutes for the big one and 20-25 minutes for the small ones, at 325°F or 170°C. While baking, initially cover the dish with aluminum foil to avoid extra browning as the quiche will be baked for about 35 minutes more with the filling.

For the Basic Cheese Custard
In a mixing bowl break the eggs and beat them until they are light. Grate the cheeses, and rub with flour. Now fold in, with a metal spoon, cheese and milk alternately into the egg. Finally fold in the cream. Your custard is now ready.

When you want to bake the quiche, get the pastry case ready. Pour $1/_3$ of the basic cheese custard into it and bake for 10 minutes at 325°F or 170°C. Remove from the oven and choose desired filling and arrange over the half-baked custard. Pour the remaining custard and bake it again for 25 minutes. It is advisable

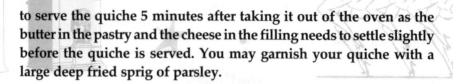

to serve the quiche 5 minutes after taking it out of the oven as the butter in the pastry and the cheese in the filling needs to settle slightly before the quiche is served. You may garnish your quiche with a large deep fried sprig of parsley.

Makes one 9.5" flan case or eight 3" individual quiches

Serves 8

Eggless Variation of Custard

ingredients

½ cup	Cheddar cheese
¼ cup	Gouda cheese
200 gms	Fresh cream
1 cup	Full fat milk
1 tbsp	Plain flour
1 tbsp	Corn flour
½ tsp	Baking powder
	Salt, pepper, mustard and nutmeg to taste

method

Mix all the ingredients in a large mixing bowl and follow the same method as above.

POTATO GRATIN DAUPHINOIS

ingredients

1 kg	Potatoes
25 gms	Butter
2 cups	Single cream
1 tsp	Nutmeg
	Salt and pepper to taste

method

Peel the potatoes and slice them very thin and soak them in very cold water for 15 minutes. Drain the and pat them dry. Preheat the oven to 300ºF or 150ºC. Melt the butter into a shallow heatproof dish. Place a layer of the potatoes in the dish. Season with salt, pepper and nutmeg. Then begin the next layer and continue the same way seasoning each layer as you go on. There should be at least 4-5 layers. Pour the cream over the dish and leave it for a few minutes so that the cream sinks down. Place the dish in the oven and let it cook slowly for approximately 30 minutes. Serve hot.

Note The slow method of cooking allows the potatoes to soak up the cream and they become tender. If cooked at higher temperature, the cream may curdle.

MOULIN ROUGE

CHEESE SOUFFLÉ

The word soufflé in French means, 'to blow air'. This is a dish that has a lot of air blown into it and can be served as a light and tasty appetizer or a main course.

ingredients

3	Eggs, separated and at room temperature
4 oz(100gms)	Strong cheese, coarsely grated
2 tbsp	Butter
2 tbsp	Plain flour
1½ cups	Milk
	Salt and pepper to taste
	Grated Parmesan cheese to dust the dishes
	A little butter to grease the dishes

* You will require individual soufflé dishes, 3½" in diameter or 1 large dish 8" in diametre.

method

Thoroughly butter the soufflé dish and dust it with grated Parmesan cheese and set aside. Preheat the oven to 400ºF or 200ºC. Make a roux with butter and flour in a saucepan. Add milk bit by bit, stirring well. Cook for 2 minutes, stirring constantly. Take it off the heat and stir in the cheese. Make sure the cheese melts thoroughly. Allow the mixture to cool and then beat in the egg yolks and season with salt and pepper, keeping extra provision for the egg whites that will be used later on. Half an hour before you want to serve, beat the egg whites until stiff enough to hold a peak. Do not over beat. Gently fold in $\frac{1}{3}$ of the beaten egg whites to the yolk mixture, scooping the sauce up from the bottom of the saucepan and turning it over. Add the rest of the egg whites and pour the mixture into the prepared dishes, place in the centre of the oven and bake for 20 minutes. (for

MOULIN ROUGE

the small dishes) and 30 minutes (for the large dish). The soufflé is done when it has risen to twice its height and is brown on the top. The soufflé sinks very quickly once out of the oven therefore it should be served immediately.

Variations on the Cheese Soufflé

- Spinach soufflé - Add 4 tbsp of spinach purée to the milk before making the sauce and reduce the cheese to 50 gms.
- Tomato soufflé - Add 1½ cup thick tomato juice instead of milk to which 1 crushed clove of garlic is added. Reduce the cheese to 50 gms.
- Soufflé fines herbs - Add 1 tbsp each of chopped parsley, mint, basil and chives to butter in a blender and use this butter to make the roux. Then proceed same as for the cheese soufflé, except use 50 gms of Parmesan cheese.
- Onion soufflé - Purée 2-3 onions and add then to ¾ cup of milk and make the sauce with it OR deep fry 2-3 onions chopped long and place them at the bottom of the dish and pour the cheese soufflé mixture over it and bake.

MOULIN ROUGE

BASIC CRÊPE RECIPE

ingredients

2	Eggs
½ tsp	Salt OR
1 tbsp	Sugar with a pinch of salt
100 gms (½ cup)	Whole wheat flour (sieved)
300 ml (½ pint)	Milk
2 tbsp	Butter, melted
	Oil for frying

method

Beat the eggs with salt or sugar and then stir in the sieved flour. Pour the milk in and beat it to a thin smooth cream, adding a little extra milk if necessary. Set aside to rest for 20 minutes. Put a thick-based frying pan, about 7" in diameter over moderate heat and brush it with oil. Pour 2 tbsp of the batter into the pan and swirl it around so that the mixture spreads evenly over the base of the pan. Let it cook for 3-4 minutes and turn it over gently with a spatula and cook on the other side. The pan shouldn't be too hot before you pour the butter. Continue until all the mixture is used up. Place the prepared crêpes on a large lightly buttered plate and cover them with butter paper, until ready to use.

Makes 12-15 6" diameter crêpes

CRÊPES GRUYÈRE

ingredients

12	Crêpes from the basic recipe
150 gms	Gruyère cheese
1½ cups	Béchamel sauce (recipe follows)
1 tbsp	Kirsch (Cherry liqueur)
4 tbsp	Fresh breadcrumbs
2 tbsp	Chopped Parsley
	A little extra grated cheese for sprinkling

method

Set the oven at 200° C. heat the Béchamel sauce and stir in the cheese and kirsch. Place a little of the warmed mixture on each crêpe and then roll them up. place them in a hot, well buttered ovenproof dish and sprinkle with breadcrumbs and grated cheese. Bake in a hot oven for 10-15 minutes. Sprinkle with chopped parsley and serve.

MOULIN ROUGE

Asparagus Crêpes

ingredients

12	Crêpes from the basic recipe
24	Asparagus spears (canned or fresh)
1½ cups	Béchamel sauce
175 gms	Cheddar cheese, grated
	Salt, pepper and mustard for seasoning

method

Cook fresh asparagus in boiling water, or drain Canned asparagus. Heat the Béchamel sauce. Add half the cheese. Season well with salt, pepper and mustard. Simmer for 2 minutes. Place 2 drained asparagus spears on each crêpe and pour 2 tbsp of the sauce over it. Roll up and arrange them side by side in an ovenproof dish. Sprinkle the remaining grated cheese on top and place under a hot grill until the cheese is golden and bubbling. Serve at once.

Serves 6-8

MOULIN ROUGE

CORN AND PEPPER CRÊPES

ingredients

12	Crêpes from the basic recipe
1½ cups	American corn, boiled and crushed
½	Green pepper, finely chopped
½	Red pepper, finely chopped
4-5 cloves	Garlic, crushed
4	Spring onions, finely chopped
2 tbsp	Butter
1½ cups	Béchamel sauce
150 gms	Cheddar cheese, grated

method

Heat butter in a saucepan and fry garlic for a minute. Add the peppers and continue cooking for 3-4 minutes. Then add corn, salt and pepper. Mix well. Take it off the stove and add the cheese and enough Béchamel sauce to coat the vegetables and gently heat it again. Use this to fill the crêpes as described in asparagus crêpe recipe

BASIC CRÊPES – EGGLESS

ingredients

100 gms	Whole wheat flour
300 ml (½ pint)	Milk
½ tsp	Salt OR
1 tbsp	Sugar + A pinch of salt
1 tsp	Baking powder
4 tbsp	Butter, melted
	Oil for frying

method

Sieve together the flour, sugar or salt and baking powder. Mix this with milk to make the batter. Add melted butter and make the crêpes as directed in the basic recipe. Set aside, covered with greaseproof paper to avoid drying.

BÉCHAMEL SAUCE

ingredients

1 cup	Milk
½ cup	Cream
1 tsp	Plain flour
1 tsp	Butter
	Salt, pepper and mustard to taste
	A pinch of nutmeg

method

In a saucepan heat butter on medium heat, add plain flour and stir for 2-3 minutes. Take it off the stove, add milk, stirring all the time. Make sure there are no lumps. Return to heat, season with salt, pepper, mustard and nutmeg. Bring to a boil, add the cream and mix well. Take it off the stove and let it cool.

Makes 1½ cups

MOULIN ROUGE

Switzerland's cuisine is varied and the products used often differ in quality. Here I have given the most popular vegetarian dishes of Swiss cuisine. The recipes include milk, butter, cheese and cream from the Alps, fruits and vegetables from the lake areas, and ofcourse, the most famous and finest chocolates in the world. So let's enjoy some of the good things in life, which can be cherished by all of us and never forgotten.

Swiss Cuisine

TRADITIONAL CHEESE FONDUE

ingredients

225 gms	Emmenthal cheese
225 gms	Gruyère cheese
2 tsp	Corn flour
2 tsp	Plain flour
2 cups	White wine
2 tbsp	Kirsch (cherry liqueur)
1 tsp	Butter
2 cloves	Garlic, crushed
	Salt and chilli powder to taste

To Serve
1 loaf	Crusty bread cut into ½" cubes

method

Place the fondue dish on the stove, melt the butter and add the garlic. Once it starts sizzling, add the wine. At the side, grate both the cheese. Add the corn flour and plain flour to them and toss lightly. When the wine starts to boil, add the cheese mixture little by little, stirring constantly in the form of 8 to avoid it sticking to the bottom of the vessel. Continue until all the cheese is incorporated. Simmer and keep stirring. Add kirsch, salt and chilli powder. Serve hot. Keep the fondue warm on a burner. Serve with warmed crusty bread cubes.

Opposite (clockwise)
i) Traditional Cheese Fondue
ii) Baby Potatoes iii) Crusty Bread

variations for the fondue

- You can add ½ a cup of pizza sauce to the wine when it is boiling before adding the cheese. Serve this with toasted strips of pizza base.
- You can add sautéed mushrooms when the fondue is ready.
- You can add tomato juice instead of wine for tomato fondue and sprinkle finely chopped basil leaves for extra flavour.
- You can add ½ a cup of chopped onions, tomatoes and green chillies to the wine when it is boiling before adding the cheese.

accompaniments for the fondue

BABY POTATOES

ingredients

½ kg	Small potatoes
2 tbsp	Olive oil
1 tbsp	Freshly chopped parsley (optional)
	Garlic salt to taste

method

Parboil the potatoes, remove the skin and set aside. In a thick non-stick pan, heat the oil. Add the garlic salt, parsley and potatoes. Cook on a slow flame for 8-10 minutes until the potatoes are slightly brown. Serve hot as an accompaniment to the fondue or for dipping in the fondue.

Opposite (clockwise)
i) Röesti Potatoes ii) Asparagus Corn Puffs
iii) Broccoli and Roasted Pepper Salad

Mushroom

ingredients

2 pkts (400 gms)	Mushrooms
2 tbsp	Olive oil
1 tbsp	Butter
3-4 cloves	Garlic, chopped
3 tbsp	Fresh cream
1 cup	White wine mixed with 1 tbsp wheat flour
	A pinch of dried mixed herbs
	Salt and pepper to taste

method

Clean and wash the mushrooms, cut into halves and set aside. In a large frying pan, heat the olive oil and butter and fry the garlic and herbs for 1 minute. Add the washed and cut mushrooms, wine and flour mixture, salt and pepper. Stirring occasionally, cook until the mushrooms are soft. At the end, all the liquid should have evaporated and the mushrooms should be soft. Add fresh cream and serve hot as an accompaniment to the fondue or any other main dish.

Serves 4-6

Asparagus And Corn Puffs

ingredients

1 cup	Chopped fresh asparagus
1 cup	Fresh corn kernels
1	Red pepper
1 tbsp	Butter
1 tbsp	Plain flour
¾ cup	Milk
3-4 tbsp	Fresh cream
1 cup	Grated cheese
¼ Kg	Puff biscuits
	Salt, pepper and mustard to taste

method

Boil the asparagus and corn separately and set aside. Chop the red pepper finely. In a saucepan, melt the butter add flour to it and cook well for 2-3 minutes. Take it off the stove and add milk, mix well to leave no lumps. Return it to the stove, add cream and half the cheese. Add the vegetables and keep the mixture warm. When you want to serve, divide each biscuit into 2 halves, place them in an oven heated to 350°F for 5 minutes. Remove from the oven, put 1 tbsp of the mixture on each half of the biscuit with a little grated cheese and serve at once.

BELL PEPPER DIABOLOTINS
Circles of Bread Covered with Cheese

ingredients

½	Red or yellow pepper, finely chopped
75 gms	Butter
3 tbsp	Plain flour
1 cup	Milk
½ tsp (each)	Salt and pepper
1 cup	Cheddar cheese, grated
½ cup	Parmesan cheese, grated
6 slices	Day old bread, sliced to medium thickness

method

Cut a 3" circle out of each slice of bread. Using half the butter, butter the circles and set them aside. In a medium sized saucepan, melt the remaining butter over moderately low heat. Remove the pan from the heat and stir in the flour to make a smooth paste. Gradually add the milk. Return the pan to the heat and bring the sauce to a boil until it becomes thick and smooth. Add the chopped pepper, salt, pepper and cheese. Beat vigorously until the cheese has melted. Arrange the buttered circles on the grill rack, spoon the cheese sauce onto them and sprinkle with Parmesan. Grill for 3-4 minutes or until browned. Serve immediately.

Makes 24 appetizer servings

RÖESTI POTATOES

ingredients

450 gms	Large potatoes
75 gms	Butter, softened
	Salt and pepper to taste

method

Peel the potatoes and grate them coarsely. Melt half the butter in a thick bottomed or a non-stick pan (with diameter of approx. 8 inches). Lightly season the grated potatoes, turn the heat up and put the potatoes in the pan. Keep pressing them down and bring them in from the edge of the pan. You need to make all the pieces of potato stick together and form a cake; at the same time keep easing the lowest portion of the potatoes to ensure that nothing is sticking to the base. Cook for about 5 minutes and dot the remaining butter on top. Turn the cake over and press it down. Cook for 5 more minutes and serve immediately.

variation

PIZZA RÖESTI

After you turn over the cake, put a layer of pizza sauce and top it with cheese. Cook for about 5-7 minutes more and serve immediately.

BROCCOLI AND ROASTED PEPPER SALAD

ingredients

1 each	Red and yellow pepper
1 large clove	Garlic, finely chopped
10-12	Olives
3 stems	Spring onions, finely chopped
1 tbsp	Chopped parsley
1 tbsp	Chopped oregano
½ kg	Broccoli florets
¼ cup	Sun-dried tomatoes, soaked for ½ an hour
6-8 tbsp	Olive oil
1 tsp	Balsamic vinegar
	Salt, pepper and crushed red pepper to taste

method

Pre heat the oven to 400°F. Cut the peppers into thin strips and toss them with 3-4 tbsp of olive oil. Set them on a baking tray, roast them till the skin is wrinkled. When cool, scrape off the skin and mix with garlic, 4 tbsp of olive oil, spring onions, tomatoes, parsley and the seasoning, and set aside. Boil 2 litres of water and drop the broccoli flowerets into it with 1 tbsp of salt and cook for 2-3 minutes. Drain on a tea towel and cool. Combine the broccoli with the rest of the salad and toss together. Adjust the salt and dribble vinegar just before serving.

The food of Spain, gentle, well seasoned and tasty, does not burn the tongue. It has its own character, better savoured than described, using as it does lemons, olives, garlic, herbs and other seasonings. Though the variety in vegetarian food is limited, I have tried to cover the maximum possible.

Spanish Cuisine

CLASSIC GAZPACHO

ingredients

For the Soup

1	Small onion, chopped
2 cloves	Garlic
3 tbsp	Olive oil
¼ cup	Red wine vinegar
1 kg	Tomatoes (dropped in hot water, put through a sieve, and boiled with 1 seasoning cube and cooled)
¼ cup	Chopped cucumber
¼ cup	Chopped red pepper
¼ cup	Chopped coriander
	Salt, pepper and lemon juice to taste

For the Accompaniments

½ cup	Finely chopped cucumber
½ cup	Finely chopped green pepper
2 sticks	Finely chopped celery
½ cup	Finely chopped hard boiled egg (optional)
1 cup	Onion and garlic flavoured croutons
2-3 tbsp	Finely chopped fresh chives

To Serve
Tabasco and Worcestershire sauce

method

Purée the first four ingredients for the soup in a liquidiser, add the sieved tomatoes, cucumber, pepper, coriander and blend to mix well. You could use additional tomato juice along with some ice cubes to thin it if you wish. Season well. Transfer the mixture to a large bowl and chill for 1-6 hours. Get all the accompaniments ready and chill the vegetables as well. Let your guests help themselves to the accompaniments as per their choice. Serve over a bowl of ice cubes.

Opposite
Classic Gazpacho

ROASTED RED PEPPER SOUP

ingredients

4	Medium sized red peppers
4	Medium sized tomatoes
¼ cup	Oil
½ tsp	Dried marjoram
½ tsp	Dried mixed herbs
2 cloves	Garlic
1	Medium sized onion, chopped
1	Medium sized leek, sliced
250 gms	Cabbage, chopped
4 cups	Water
1 tsp	Sweet chilli sauce
	Salt and pepper to taste

To Garnish
Fresh herbs, finely chopped
Sour cream

method

Cut the red peppers into quarters. Apply a little oil onto each piece and grill until the skin blackens slightly. Allow it to cool and remove the skin. Cut the tomatoes and scoop out the seeds. In a large pan, heat the oil and add the herbs and garlic. Stir over low heat for 1 minute. Add the onions and leeks and cook for 3 minutes until golden. Add the cabbage, tomatoes, peppers and water. Bring to a boil, then reduce heat and simmer for 20 minutes. Remove from heat and allow to cool. Liquidise, add chilli sauce and season with salt and pepper. Garnish with herbs and sour cream. Serve hot.

Opposite (clockwise)
i) Vegetable Paella ii) Salad Sevillana
iii) Basque Mushroom Toast

Spinach Corquettes With Yogurt Sauce

ingredients

1 cup	Short grained rice
100 gms	Feta cheese or goat cheese
¼ cup	Grated Parmesan cheese
1	Egg, beaten OR 4 tbsp milk
1 clove	Garlic, crushed
1 tsp	Grated lemon rind
¼ cup	Finely chopped spring onions
200 gms	Spinach leaves, dropped in boiling water, drained and chopped
1 tbsp	Plain flour mixed with ¼ cup water
1½ cups	Dry breadcrumbs
	A pinch of nutmeg
	Salt and pepper to taste
	Oil for frying

For the Yogurt Sauce

200 gms	Thick yogurt
2 tbsp	Chopped fresh mint
1 tbsp	Lemon juice
1 tsp	Sugar
	Salt and pepper to taste

method

Cook the rice in 2 cups of boiling water until tender and drain. Mix together the rice, cheese, egg or milk, garlic, lemon rind, spring onion, spinach, salt, pepper and nutmeg in a bowl. Using wet hands, divide the mixture into 15 portions. Shape each portion into a cylindrical shape. Place them on a tray and refrigerate for 30 minutes.

Spread the breadcrumbs on a sheet of greaseproof paper. Dip each croquette into the flour-water mixture. Then coat with breadcrumbs, shake off the excess and refrigerate for another 30 minutes. Heat the oil in a deep pan and fry the croquettes, 4-5 at a time until they are golden and crisp. Drain on to a paper towel and serve hot with yogurt sauce.
Makes 15 croquettes

For the Sauce
Combine the yogurt, fresh mint, lemon juice sugar, salt and pepper. Mix well. Cover and chill until you want to serve.

Makes 1 cup

BASQUE MUSHROOM TOAST

ingredients

3 tbsp	Olive oil
225 gms(1 pkt)	Mushrooms, thinly sliced
1 tbsp	Plain flour
¼ cup	Dry Sherry or white wine
½	Red chilli, chopped
1 cup	Vegetable stock
¼ cup	Freshly chopped parsley
2 tbsp	Fresh cream
6-8	Thick slices of French bread

To Serve
Olive oil

method

Heat olive oil in a frying pan, add garlic and red chilli and fry for a minute. Add mushrooms and continue cooking. Mix flour with sherry or white wine in a cup and add this to the mushrooms when they are cooked yet firm. Add chopped parsley and cream. Mix well and take off the stove. Heat the bread slices and brush with olive oil. Spread the mixture evenly on the slices and serve.

Serves 6-8

SALAD SEVILLANA

ingredients

For the Dressing

1 cup	Olive oil
½ cup	Red wine vinegar
¼ cup	Onion, chopped
¼ cup	Sugar
1½ tsp	Paprika
1 tsp	Mustard
1 tsp	Salt
½ tsp	Black pepper

Combine in a blender until frothy. Cover and refrigerate

For the Salad

A choice of vegetables (fresh spinach, artichoke hearts, lettuce, avocado, white onions, olives, peppers, boiled baby potatoes, and boiled green beans). Hard-boiled eggs may also be added.

method

Combine any of the above vegetables in a large salad bowl and chill. Serve with the given dressing.

Berenjenas Patatas Et Pimentos Con Tumbet

Eggplant, Potato and Pepper Casserole in Fresh Tomato Sauce

ingredients

For the Sauce

1½ tbsp	Olive oil
1	Large onion, chopped
5 cloves	Garlic, chopped
2 stems	Fresh thyme, plucked
3½ cups	Diced tomatoes
2 level tsp	Brown sugar
1 level tsp	Oregano (dried)
	Salt and pepper to taste

For the Casserole

3	Large peppers, sliced
1 kg	Eggplant, thinly sliced with salt sprinkled over it
1 kg	Potatoes, thinly sliced
5 tbsp	Minced Fresh thyme
5-6 tbsp	Grated Cheddar cheese
	Oil for frying

method

To make the sauce, heat the oil in a saucepan. Fry the onions and garlic, add thyme and cook until onions are soft. Then add tomatoes, oregano, sugar, slat and pepper. Cook until sauce is thick and set aside.

In a large frying pan pour the oil (enough to cover the surface of the frying pan) and fry all the vegetables in batches until they are well cooked. Set aside each separately.

to assemble

Lightly grease a round casserole dish with olive oil. Arrange the sautéed potatoes at the bottom of the dish, pour the prepared tomato sauce over it evenly. Then top this with the eggplant and sauce, followed by peppers and sauce and finally sprinkle cheese and fresh thyme. Bake in a hot oven for 10-15 minutes. Serve hot.

Serves 6-8

PAELLA
Vegetable Spanish Rice

ingredients

1 ½ cups	Spanish or medium grained rice
2 tbsp	Olive oil
1	Red pepper, chopped
4 cloves	Garlic, minced with 4 red chillies
½ kg	Tomatoes (drop them into hot water, liquidise, strain and make 400ml juice)
2	Medium sized onions, chopped
1 cup	Tomato purée
3 cups	Vegetable stock
½ cup	Green peas
1	Courgette, finely chopped
½ cup	White beans, boiled
1 cup	Finely chopped green onions
1 cup	Washed and thinly sliced mushrooms
1 tsp	Sugar
½ cup	Hot water mixed with ½ tsp saffron

To Garnish
50 gms Cheddar cheese
½ green pepper, sliced
Shredded almonds
Sliced olives

method

In a large frying pan, heat the olive oil over medium heat, add onions and spring onions, garlic, chillies and red pepper, sauté until golden. Add the vegetables and cook for 5 minutes. Add the washed and soaked rice. Stir to coat with oil. Add the stock and bring to a boil. Then add tomato Purée, tomato sauce, salt and sugar. Cook until the rice is tender. Add the saffron water and cook for 5 minutes. Turn it out onto a serving plate, garnish with cheese, peppers and olives. Serve hot.

Vegetable Patties With Rich Tomato Sauce

ingredients

For the Patties

1½ cups	Mixed boiled vegetables (potato, carrot, corn, peas baby corn)
½ kg	Puff pastry
2 tsp	Oil
1	Onion, finely chopped
½ cup	Vegetable stock
1 tbsp	Finely chopped parsley
½ tsp	French or grainy mustard
2 tbsp	Butter
	Salt and pepper to taste

For the Sauce

1 tbsp	Olive oil
1	Small onion, chopped
1 clove	Garlic, crushed
2	Tomatoes, blanched and chopped
¼ cup	Red wine
¼ cup	Vegetable stock
2 tbsp	Tomato paste
½ tsp (each)	Dried basil and oregano

method

For the Patties

Heat the oil in a frying pan and cook onion over medium heat for 2 minutes. Add all the vegetables and the vegetable stock, bring to a boil. Reduce heat and cool until the liquid has evaporated. Add the parsley, salt, pepper and mustard. Mix well and leave to cool.

Roll out the pastry to 3 mm. thickness and cut into 5" circles. Place 1 tbsp of mixture onto each pastry and fold over so the edges meet to form a triangle. Twist the edges together decoratively to seal. Brush with a little butter and place patties on a greased baking sheet and bake in a preheated oven at 200°C until golden. Serve hot with rich tomato sauce.
Makes 12 Patties

For the Sauce
Heat oil in a small saucepan, add onion and garlic. Cook until soft. Add the tomatoes, wine and vegetable stock and bring to a boil. Reduce heat and simmer for 15 minutes, stirring occasionally. Remove from heat and cool. Process the tomato mixture in a liquidiser until smooth. Return to the stove, add the tomato paste, basil and oregano and stir until hot. Serve hot or cold.

CONSOMMÉ BASQUAISE
Clear Red Pepper Soup

ingredients

100 gms	Red pepper, finely chopped
1 tbsp	Butter
3 cups	Clear brown stock
4 tbsp	Boiled rice
4 tsp	Chopped oregano or parsley
	Salt and pepper

method

Melt the butter in a pan over gentle heat. Add the diced pepper and cook gently for 15 minutes. Take care to see that it doesn't burn. In the meanwhile, pour the stock into the pan and bring to a boil. Stir the hot stock into the cooked peppers. Add rice and simmer for 5 minutes. Adjust seasoning, pour into bowls and sprinkle herbs on top and serve.

Serves 4

There are icy-cold drinks and refreshing fruit punches for sunny afternoons and steaming hot beverages which are great chill removers for cold days. Here there are many interesting variations and combinations using fresh fruit, fruit juices and nectars. A fancy ice ring and garnishes like curls of lemon or orange peel and cherries give a lovely party touch. The use of the right glass gives you a perfect touch to your setting.

Desserts are devised for pleasure alone. At the end of the meal, when appetites are largely satisfied, the dessert restores the palate and hints at sensuous luxury. When you are entertaining, this is invariably the last item your guests will eat before leaving and so the impression must be favourable.

Seek out fresh ingredients like eggs, butter, cream, the finest chocolate, perfectly ripe fruits etc. They contribute to a great extent in achieving the best results. The elaborate desserts may also require the application of many techniques – pounding or sieving, beating or churning, baking or freezing. So pay attention to these techniques. But, whatever the degree of complexity, all desserts demand attention to detail. For example, to make a perfect soufflé or mousse, the egg whites must be soft enough to blend easily with a flavouring; they should be beaten only until they form gently dropping peaks. At the end of it, a good-looking dessert will be a creation not to be missed.

Here, I've tried to give you recipes, which are easy to follow and which will give you the best results – a dessert which will be complimented and will complete the meal which has gone before.

Drinks & Desserts

Margarita

ingredients

4 pegs	Tequila
2 pegs	Triple Sec or Cointreau
½ cup	Lemon juice
½ cup	Powdered sugar
¾ cup	Crushed ice
1	Egg white, stiffly beaten (optional)

* You will need 4 chilled stemmed glasses and salt in a plate.

method

Invert the glass rims in coarse salt to coat the rims evenly. Set aside. In a blender, combine Tequila, Triple Sec, lemon juice, sugar and crushed ice. Whisk until frothy and well blended. Now add the egg white and blend once more and pour into the prepared glasses.

variations

Strawberry Margarita- Add ½ cup fresh strawberry pulp and reduce lemon to ¼ cup. Blend the same way. Decorate the glasses with sliced strawberries on the rim.

Kiwi Margarita- Add ½ cup kiwi pulp or ¼ cup kiwi liqueur and ¼ cup lemon juice and proceed the same way.

Makes 4 glasses

GOLDEN AMBROSIA

ingredients

1 litre	Orange juice
750 ml	Pineapple juice
3 cups	Water
1 cup	Sugar
1 litre	Ginger ale (Canada Dry)
2	Oranges, segmented

To Garnish
Mint leaves
Lemon slices

method

Combine sugar and water. Stir over low heat until the sugar has dissolved. Mix both juices and chill. Just before serving, add chilled ginger ale and orange segments.

Note To make this into an alcoholic cocktail, take one large peg of vodka, one small peg of peach schnapps and pour the prepared mixture into the glass. Decorate with fresh mint leaves and lemon slices.

PINA COLADA

ingredients

1 large peg	Light rum
1 cup	Cream of coconut (Thick coconut milk)
2 cups	Pineapple juice
	Crushed ice

To Garnish
Pineapple slices and cherries threaded together on a cocktail stick

* You will need 4 stemmed glasses to serve in

method

Blend all the ingredients together with ice. Serve in stemmed glasses and garnish with a cherry and pineapple slice on a stick along with a straw.

Note For a Virgin Pina Colada simply omit light rum and proceed the same way.

Planter's Punch Bowl

ingredients

3 cups	Orange juice, chilled
3 cups	Pineapple juice, chilled
1 ½ cups	Lemon juice, chilled
1 cup	Fresh lime juice, chilled
1 cup	Light rum (Bacardi rum)
1 cup	Peach schnapps
½ cup	Powdered sugar
	Ice ring (recipe follows)
	Cherries, mint leaves and lemon slices
	for the Ice Ring

* You will need a Punch bowl to serve in.

method

Combine all the juices, rum and sugar in a punch bowl. Blend well. Float ice ring on the punch.

ICE RING

Choose a ring mould tin to suit your punch bowl. Place it in the freezer until well chilled. Rinse the inside with cold water; return to the freezer until a thin coating of ice forms. Arrange cherries, evenly spaced. Slowly, add enough water to cover the cherries. Freeze until firm. Arrange lemon slices directly over the cherries and add enough water to cover it. Freeze until firm. Fill the mould to the top with cold water and freeze again until firm. When ready to use, run cold water over the mould to loosen it and then unmould onto the punch bowl.

Serves 10-12

Banana Daiquiri

ingredients

1 peg	Light Rum
2 tbsp	Lemon juice
2 tbsp	Sugar, powdered
½	Medium sized ripe banana
	Finely crushed ice

* You will need 1 chilled stemmed glass

method

Place all the ingredients in a blender along with half a cup of crushed ice and blend. Immediately pour out into the chilled glass.
DO NOT STRAIN.

Serves 1

variation

Strawberry Daiquiri
Instead of the banana, use ½ cup sliced strawberries

Carnival Punch

ingredients

4 cups	Unsweetened orange juice
15	Ice cubes
2 cups	Grape fruit juice
1 cup	White grape juice
1 cup	Apple juice
1 cup	Black & white grapes washed and halved
	A few sprigs of mint

*Add 1 peg vodka or white rum per serving for an alcoholic version of this drink

method

In a large punch bowl or jug put ice cubes, add all the other ingredients, mix well. Chill for at least 15 minutes before serving in tall glasses.

Serves 10

KAHWA

ingredients

600 ml	Boiling water
4 level tsp	Green tea leaves
¼ tsp	Powdered saffron
2	Cardamoms, crushed
1 stick	Cinnamon, crushed
2	Cloves, crushed
8	Almonds, blanched and chopped
	Sugar to taste

method

In a saucepan place tea leaves and pour boiling water over them. Allow to infuse over a very low flame. Dissolve saffron in a little water by rubbing it gently. Strain the tea into another saucepan and add saffron liquid alongwith all the other ingredients.
Serve hot.

Epicure's Millennium Punch

ingredients

1 peg	Campari
1 peg	Vodka
½ peg	Cointreau
2 pegs	Lemonade or bitter lemon
2 pegs	Orange juice
1 tsp	Lemon juice
4-5	Ice cubes
1 bottle	Soda water

To Garnish
Slice of orange with the skin

method

Place ice in a very tall glass and layer all the ingredients in the given order and serve with a stirrer and an orange wedge.

Note This is an excellent poolside drink.

Serves 1

Peach Daiquiri

ingredients

½ cup	Chopped peaches
2 tbsp	Lemon juice
2 tbsp	Powdered sugar
1 peg	White rum (optional)
	Crushed ice

To Garnish
Mint sprigs
Lemon slices

* You will need 1 chilled stemmed glass

method

Put all the ingredients in a blender and blend until frothy. Pour in the chilled glass, garnish and serve.

LEMON AND LIME COOLER

ingredients

1 glass	Sweet lime juice
3 tbsp	Sugar
	Juice of ½ a lemon
	A dash of Campari

To Garnish
Lemon slices
Mint leaves

To Serve
Crushed ice

method

Mix the lemon juice and sugar until dissolved. Mix this with the sweetlime juice. Now, take 2 tall glasses, put crushed ice at the bottom, pour the lemon and lime juices over it and gently dribble the Campari over it. Do not mix. Garnish each glass with a lemon slice and mint leaves and serve.

Makes 2 glasses

BERRY TANG

ingredients

¼ cup	Cranberry, black berry or strawberry juice
1 tbsp	Lemon juice
200 ml	Tonic water (1 bottle)
	Ice cubes

To Garnish
Slice of lemon
Mint leaves

method

Mix the juice together in a tall glass. Add 4-5 ice cubes and top it up with tonic water. Garnish and serve immediately.

SANGRIA

ingredients

8 oz	Water
½ cup	Rock sugar
1 tsp	Cinnamon
2	Oranges, sliced
1	Lemon, sliced
1 bottle	Medium-dry red wine
3 oz	Brandy (optional)
	Fresh fruit, chopped (optional)

method

Combine water, sugar and cinnamon in a saucepan. Cook over moderate heat until the ingredients dissolve into a syrup. Put sliced fruits into a bowl, and pour the syrup over it. Allow to stand for four or more hours, at room temperature. When you want to serve, place ice cubes in a large pitcher. Add the syrup and fruit and top it with wine and brandy if used. Stir until pitcher is frosted. Add chopped fresh fruit on top, and serve chilled.

Makes 6 glasses

VENETIAN COFFEE

ingredients

1½ tsp	Instant coffee powder
1 tsp	Coffee liqueur (Tia Maria or Kahlua)
1 cup	Boiling water
1	Small scoop vanilla ice-cream
	Sugar to taste

To Sprinkle
Cinnamon and chocolate powder

* You will need a stemmed glass and a coffee spoon to serve

method

In a wine-glass, put in the coffee powder and a metal spoon (to avoid cracking the glass). Pour the boiling water over it, add the coffee liqueur and very gently scoop ice cream onto the top. Sprinkle cinnamon and chocolate powder according to individual taste. Serve immediately.

Pimm's No.1

ingredients

30 ml	Pimm's No.1
15 ml	Vodka (optional)
150 ml	Lemonade
60 ml	Soda
2-3 tbsp	Chopped mixed fruits (apple, pear, kiwi, sweet lime, orange, banana etc.)
	A dash of lemon juice
	Ice cubes
	A few mint leaves

method

Pour the Pimm's and Vodka into a tall serving glass. Add lemonade and soda. Mix well. Top it up with fruits, mint leaves and ice.

Serves 1

MINT AND LEMON ICED TEA

ingredients

4 cups	Water
4	Tea bags
	Ice cubes and Sugar cubes
	The juice of 4 lemons
	A fistful of mint leaves

method

Combine the tea bags and water in a glass pitcher. Set aside for 1-6 hours. Remove the tea bags. Add sugar and lemon and top it up with ice cubes and mint. Serve chilled.

GÂTEAU MOUNT BLANC

ingredients

For the Choux Pastry (Profiteroles)

7½ fl oz/200 ml	Water
2½ oz or 65 ml	Butter
3¾ oz or 100 ml	Plain flour, well sieved
3	Eggs, beaten
	A pinch of salt
	A pinch of sugar
1 tsp	Vanilla

For the Cream Filling

300 gms	Fresh cream
½ tsp	Vanilla essence
5 tbsp	Powdered sugar
1½ tbsp	Kirsch (optional)

For the Chocolate Sauce

200 gms	Semi sweet cooking chocolate
¾ cup	Milk + cream , mixed
50 gms	Butter
2 tbsp	Icing sugar
¼ cup	Additional cream, if required
1 tsp	Vanilla essence

method

For the Choux Pastry

Pre heat the oven to 180°C. In a heavy saucepan, bring water to boil, along with salt and butter. As soon as the liquid rises, like milk, remove from heat and add sugar and vanilla. Add the flour all at once and beat vigorously with a wooden spoon to obtain a smooth paste. Return onto low heat till the mixture dries out. Make sure it doesn't stick to the pan. Remove from heat and allow it to cool. Using a rotary beater, beat in the egg liquid little by little until all the egg has been absorbed thoroughly.

Opposite
Gâteau Mount Blanc

Make sure the mixture does not become runny. Butter the baking sheet lightly. Fill the icing bag with the pastry and pipe the profiteroles in a diameter of 2 cm. Keep a little space between them to rise. Bake for 20-25 minutes. Do not open the oven in the first 15 minutes or else the choux will collapse. Remove from the oven once they are firm and golden. Leave to cool on a wire rack.

Makes 30 profiteroles

For the Cream Filling
In order to whip the cream successfully, it must be whisked in a very cold stainless steel bowl in a cool place. Pour in the cold cream in the bowl. Whip it with a whisk, if necessary place the bowl over ice cubes. When the cream starts to thicken, add sugar, one spoon at a time. Add vanilla and kirsch. If not used immediately, refrigerate until use.

For the Chocolate Sauce
Break the chocolate into pieces, melt gently in a double boiler. When melted, transfer it into a heavy saucepan, and add the cream-milk mixture, butter and vanilla. Allow to cool. Add sugar and mix well. Add additional whipped cream if the sauce is too liquid.

Makes 1½ cups Chocolate Sauce

assembling the gateau

Slit each profirterole with a knife; fill the whipped cream in it with a piping bag. Pile up the profiteroles like a mountain on a deep serving plate, using warm chocolate sauce to pour over and in the end, pipe the tip of the pile with cream. Chill for several hours. Serve with the remaining chocolate sauce at the side.

Opposite (right to left)
i) Mint and Lemon Iced Tea ii) Strawberry Diaquiri
iii) Venetian Coffee

TIRAMISU

Tiramisu is a cool, refreshing Italian dessert that was initially created in Sienna, a north western province of Tuscany. The word 'tiramisu' means pick me up. It is a very light, mocha flavoured, whipped cream concoction with sheets of sponge cake soaked in strong coffee and has a tantalizing hint of liqeuer. Suddenly, you experience a tiny explosion of chocolate on your tongue but it disappears in a flash. This great dessert is like heaven in your mouth leaving a tingling sensation on your tastebuds.

ingredients

250 gms	Mascarpone cheese
3	Egg yolks
2	Egg whites
6 tbsp	Sugar
$1/_3$ cup	Marsala or sherry
½ cup	Fresh cream
¼ kg	Sponge cake
2 tbsp	Kahlua
2 tsp	Camp coffee essence
½ cup	Strong coffee

To Garnish
Chocolate powder
Chocolate shavings

method

Slice the sponge cake into thin sheets, toast them lightly and set aside.

Make a zabaglione by beating the egg yolk and sugar in the top of a double boiler until it turns ivory coloured. Add marsala and whisk over simmering water until the mixture begins to thicken. Allow it to cool slightly. Add ¼cup coffee to the mascarpone with 3 tbsp with 3 tbsp sugar. Beat it into the zabaglione mixture. Whip the cream to soft peaks and fold it into the zabaglione mixture gently. Beat the egg whites until stiff, fold into the mixture as well. Set aside till you assemble. Mix the remaining coffee with Kahlua and camp coffee and soak the toasted sponge cake sheets in this. If you wish to serve this set it in a bowl. Line a transparent glass bowl or wine glasses for individual servings with sponge cake sheets. Pour the zabaglione mixture over it to cover all the cake till about ½ an inch high. Again layer the sponge cake sheets alternately with the mixture up to the brim of the glass or a bowl. Finish with cream on the top. Cover and freeze for 6-8 hours. Just before serving, garnish with chocolate powder and shavings. Serve chilled.

Note If you wish to unmould this dessert after it has set, then you have to set it in an aluminium tin, freeze it overnight and invert on to a serving platter and then decorate as you like.

EGGLESS TIRAMISU

ingredients

200 gms	Mascarpone cheese
200 gms	Fresh cream
½ cup	Powdered sugar
½ cup	Strong coffee
250 gms	Sponge cake, slice into thin sheets and then toasted
2 tbsp	Coffee liqueur Kahlua or Irish cream (optional)
2 tsp	Camp coffee essence

To Garnish
Grated and powdered chocolate

method

Whip the cream in a chilled bowl with chilled beaters. Combine the mascarpone and powdered sugar and beat for 2 minutes with the beater at medium speed. Then add ¼ cup of coffee and continue beating. Do not over beat. Mix the Kahlua and coffee essence into the strong coffee. Fold the whipped cream into the Mascarpone mixture. Take the toasted sponge cake sheets and soak them in the coffee mixture and line the serving bowl or individual glasses with them. Pour the Mascarpone mixture over it and alternate with sponge sheets,the last layer being that of the cheese mixture. Freeze of 4 - 6 hours. Garnish with grated and powdered chocolate and serve chilled.

Serves 6

Double Chocolate Chip Ice Cream

ingredients

3½ oz (90 gms)	Plain chocolate, broken into pieces + 2 tbsp cocoa
½ pint	Milk
3	Egg yolks
3 oz(75 gms)	Sugar
300 gms	Fresh cream
2½ oz(65 gms)	Chocolate, chopped

method

Stir the chocolate pieces and cocoa with milk in a saucepan over low heat, until the chocolate melts and the mixture is smooth. Whisk the egg yolks with the sugar in a mixing bowl, until the mixture falls off the whisk in a thick ribbon. Gradually add the chocolate flavoured milk, whisking constantly. Pour the mixture back into the saucepan and stir over medium heat, until it thickens and coats the back of the spoon. Strain into a bowl and cool in the refrigerator. When cold, fold in the whipped cream. Pour the mixture into a churner, add the chopped chocolate and churn until set.

Note For the eggless variation, replace egg yolks with 6 tbsp condensed milk.

COFFEE ROULADE

ingredients

For the Roulade

4	Eggs, separated
4 oz	Castor sugar
4 oz	Plain flour, well sieved + ½tsp baking powder + a pinch of salt
3 tbsp	Warm water
1 tbsp	Camp coffee essence

* You will need a 12″ x 8″ x ½″ deep tray lined with greaseproof paper and coated with melted butter.

For the Filling

400 gms	Fresh cream
3-4 tbsp	Sugar
1 tbsp	Camp coffee
2 tbsp	Instant coffee mixed with 1 tbsp hot water
1 tbsp	Kahlua or Tia Maria (optional)

To Garnish

Flakes of almond or chocolate pieces

method

For the Roulade

Preheat the oven to 180°C. Slightly warm the bowl in which you place the egg yolks and beat with an electric mixer for 5 minutes. Then add the sugar little by little, beating well after each addition. Now turn down the speed of your mixer (to number 1) and gently fold in the flour mixture alternating it with water. Beat gently until all the mixture is absorbed. Take the beaters off and clean them.

With dry beaters, beat the egg whites till stiff and fold in with a metal spoon in a circular motion till all the whites are absorbed. Quickly pour into the prepared tray and bake in the oven for about 15-18 minutes. Do not over bake or else it will not roll. Now turn it out onto sugared foil or a dampened tea towel and roll it gently. Let it cool.

For the Filling
Beat the cream till thick, add sugar, coffee essence, instant coffee and Kahlua. Continue beating till thick.

Now open up the roulade and spread the flavored cream onto it and re roll carefully. Garnish with flakes of almond and chocolate pieces. Transfer to a serving tray. Chill until ready to serve.

MOCCA CREAM
Layered Coffee Cake

ingredients

1	8-9 inch plain sponge cake
1 cup	Butter
2½ cups	Powdered sugar
2 tbsp	Camp coffee or vanilla essence
3 tbsp	Instant coffee powder
1 cup	Hot water
¼ cup	Almond flakes, roasted

method

Get the cake a day before you want to use it and refrigerate. Cut the cake horizontally into very thin slices. You should get 6-7 slices out of one cake. Set aside. Make coffee decoction by mixing hot water with instant coffee and essence. Let the water cool. Now start beating butter with the rotary beater until light and fluffy. Add the sugar spoon by spoon alternating with 1 small spoon of the coffee decoction until all the sugar is incorporated and the mixture is light and fluffy and is of spreading consistency. Now take the bottom layer of the cake and place it on the serving dish and soak it with the coffee decoction. Spread a thin layer of the coffee cream, even it out with a spatula. Place another slice of cake over it carefully, making sure that it is exactly in line with the first and repeat the earlier procedure until all the slices are used. After the last layer, frost the whole cake with the remaining coffee cream. Even it out and sprinkle the roasted almonds on top. Serve at room temperature.

Serves 6-8

Strawberry Meringue Pie

ingredients

For the Meringue

3	Egg whites
170gms OR 6oz	Half castor and half icing sugar, sieved
	A pinch of cream of tartar

For the Filling

500 gms	Strawberries
200 gms	Fresh cream
1 tsp	Lemon juice
2 tbsp	Icing sugar
1 tsp	Strawberry liqueur (optional)

method

For the Meringue

Whisk the egg whites until stiff, add cream of tartar. Fold in the sugar gradually, beat until all the sugar is incorporated properly. Pipe or spoon the mixture onto a well oiled or buttered baking tray to 8 inch round size. Bake it in an oven at 110ºC or 220ºF or gas mark 1 for 2-3 hours, until crisp. Take care that it should be off-white and not brown. Remove from the baking sheet with a warmed palette knife. Cool and store in an air tight container until used.

For the Filling

Wash and clean the strawberries and crush them with a fork, reserving 2-3 for the top. Beat the cream in a chilled stainless steel bowl with icing sugar and strawberry liqueur and lemon juice. Keep both these chilled until use.

To Serve

When you want to serve, place the meringue shell onto a serving plate. Mix strawberries with cream spread over the shell and decorate with sliced strawberries.
Serve immediately.

LEMON MERINGUE PIE

ingredients

For the Sweet Flan Pastry

100 gms	Butter, melted and lukewarm	
200 gms	Plain flour	
½ tsp	Salt	} Sieve
1 tbsp	Powdered sugar	together
	Grated rind of 1 lemon	
1 tbsp	Fresh cream	} Beat
	1 egg	together

* You will need a 10 inch Pie dish

For the Filling

	Juice of 5 lemons
4 level tbsp	Plain flour
2 level tbsp	Corn flour
¾ cups	Water
240 gms	Powdered sugar
4	Egg yolks
1 tbsp	Butter

For the Meringue

3	Egg whites
100 gms	Icing sugar
2 tbsp	Lemon juice OR 1 tbsp juice and
	1 tbsp lemon essence
	A pinch of salt
	A pinch of cream of tartar

To Serve

Vanilla ice cream or Whipped cream

method

Pre heat the oven to 180°C. Place flour mixture in a bowl, make a well in the centre. Put in the butter and rub with your fingertips. When the mixture resembles breadcrumbs, add the egg and cream mixture and make a soft dough. Cover it and chill in the fridge for an hour. Remove and roll out the pastry very lightly to fit in the 10″ pie dish. Prick it with a fork and bake blindly for 25 minutes in the middle rack or until the pastry is golden.

In the meantime, make the lemon curd. Mix together the flour, corn flour, water and lemon juice, beating with a whisk. Gradually bring it to a boil, beating all the time. Add sugar little by little, stirring continuously, remove from heat. Cool slightly. Beat together egg yolks and butter. Add to the lukewarm mixture and whisk until it becomes thicker. Set aside.

Remove the pastry from the oven, but leave the oven on at 180°C. Pour lemon curd over the pastry and prepare the meringues. In a bowl put in the egg whites and salt. Beat, starting slowly and gradually increasing the speed, once the eggs are stiff add sugar slowly, a spoon at a time till all the sugar is incorporated. Add essence or lemon juice and fold in gently with a spatula. Place in a piping bag and pipe over the pie with it. Cook in the middle rack of the oven for approximately 10 minutes until the meringue is light brown. Serve at room temperature with whipped cream or vanilla ice cream.

SHORTCAKE BASE FOR EGGLESS DESSERT

ingredients

225 gms	Whole meal or plain flour
½ tsp	Cinnamon, ground
1 tbsp	Baking powder
1 tsp	Salt
75 gms	Butter
250 ml 8 fl oz	Milk

method

Set the oven at 200ºC or 400ºF. Sift together flour, cinnamon, baking powder and salt. Rub in the butter until the mixture resembles fine breadcrumbs. Add the milk and mix to form a soft dough. Divide the dough into two and roll it out and line two well oiled 8" round tins. Bake in the preheated oven for 15 minutes. Remove and cool on a wire rack. Place one short cake on a serving plate and cover with the strawberries and cream mixture. Top with another short cake, piped cream and strawberries on the top.

Serves 6-8

Orange Sorbet

ingredients

3½ cups	Fresh orange juice, strained (8-10 oranges)
200 gms	Sugar
	Juice of 3 lemons

method

When you extract the orange juice, put the pulp of 2-3 oranges through a blender and add this to the juice. Mix sugar with the juice, stirring with a wooden spoon until the sugar dissolves. Pour the mixture into a copper bottomed stainless steel pan and freeze. You must prevent crystallization during freezing. Freeze the mixture for 1 hour, remove and cut lumps. Put these through the food processor until completely smooth. Repeat 2-3 times. When the sorbet is nearly frozen, take it out, beat well and put it back into the freezer in the mould you wish to use. Freeze for 30 minutes. This way the sorbet will not turn into hard ice cubes. Scoop it out with an ice cream serving spoon and serve in stemmed glasses.

STRAWBERRY MOUSSE

ingredients

3	Eggs
2	Egg yolks
100 gms	Powdered sugar, sieved
300 gms	Double cream
225 gms	Strawberries
2 tbsp	Brandy or lemon juice
15 gms	Gelatine mixed with 5 tbsp liquid

To Decorate
5-6 Sliced strawberries and ¼ cup whipped cream

method

Break eggs in a big bowl (3 eggs and 2 egg yolks) and beat at high speed for at least 5 minutes. Then add the sugar spoon by spoon and continue to beat for 7 more minutes. Transfer this mixture to another bigger bowl. Beat the cream to a thick consistency. Liquidise the cleaned strawberries with icing sugar and brandy or lemon juice, which is then reduced on the stove down to 5 fl oz or 150 ml and then cool it. Combine the cream with the strawberry mixture and it should be whipped enough to merge with the egg mixture. Fold it into the egg mixture in circular movements. Then fold in the gelatine at the end and pour this into a 1½ litre size big or small individual bowls and chill in the refrigerator. Decorate before serving with slices of strawberries and whipped cream.

Orange Soufflé

ingredients

450 gms	Orange segments
2 cups	Milk
5 tbsp	Powdered sugar
6 tsp	Custard powder
¾ tsp	Orange essence
2½ tbsp	Gelatine
1 tbsp	Sugar
1 cup	Fresh orange juice
2 tbsp	Lemon juice
300 gms	Cream
5 tbsp	Powdered sugar
	A few drops of orange colouring (optional)

method

Combine the milk and sugar in a saucepan and heat. Dissolve the custard powder in a little cold milk and add to the hot milk. Stir until thick. Remove from heat and cool. Mix in the orange essence and colouring. Then mix together the gelatine and sugar. Add the orange juice, put it to boil on a slow flame and then add lemon juice. When the gelatine is completely dissolved, take it off the stove and beat it over a bowl of ice cubes with an electric beater until fluffy and creamy. Beat the fresh cream in a chilled stainless steel bowl and gradually add powdered sugar. Keep beating over ice until stiff. Separate the orange segments slightly, keeping 8-10 intact for decoration. Take a big bowl, place it over the ice cubes. Mix in the cooled custard, cream, beaten gelatine mixture and orange segments. Mix well. Keep it over the ice, scraping the sides until the soufflé becomes thick. Pour this into a serving bowl and allow it to set for about 3-4 hours or overnight. Just before serving, pipe some cream and arrange orange segments on the top.

Nougat Basket

ingredients

½ cup	Cashew nuts	coarsely powdered
½ cup	Peanuts,	without the skin
1 ½ cups	Sugar	
2 tsp	Sugar, for the handle	
	A little oil	

To Serve
Vanilla or Butterscotch ice cream and chopped fresh fruits

method

Place the sugar in a very thick vessel and put it on the stove and slowly let the sugar dissolve, stirring from time to time. Add the nuts, mix well and take the mixture off the stove immediately. Oil a slab or working surface, 2 knives and a bowl. Pour the mixture on the slab or working surface and work it with 2 knives until it forms a dough. Take ¾ of it and roll it thinly and as quickly as possible. Press this rolled dough into the oiled bowl to form a basket in the shape of the bowl. Let it cool and remove it very gently. Then, place it over a serving plate or keep it in an airtight container until used. To make the handle of the basket, roll out the remaining dough. If it has hardened, re-heat it slightly. Roll it out into a long strip that you then bend like a U while hot. Melt 2 tsp of sugar in a small vessel, dip the ends of the strip in it and stick it firmly to the bowl to form a handle. Fill your nougat basket with ice cream or fresh fruit and serve.

Serves 10

Basic Crêpes Recipe

ingredients

2	Eggs
1 tbsp	Sugar with a pinch of salt
100 gms (½ cup)	Whole wheat flour (sieved)
300 ml (½ pint)	Milk
2 tbsp	Butter, melted
1 tbsp	Grand Mariner (orange liqueur) (optional)
	Oil for frying

method

Beat the eggs with salt and sugar and then stir in the sieved flour. Pour the milk in and beat it to a thin smooth cream. You could add 3 tbsp Grand Mariner if you wish. Set aside to rest for 20 minutes. Put a thick-based frying pan, about 7" in diameter on moderate heat and brush it with oil. Pour 2 tbsp of the batter into the pan and swirl it around so that the mixture spreads evenly over the base of the pan. Let it cook for 3-4 minutes and turn it over gently with a spatula and cook the other side. The pan shouldn't be too hot before you pour in the batter. Continue until all the mixture is used up. Place the prepared crêpes on a large lightly buttered plate and cover them with butter paper, until ready to use.

CRÊPES SUZETTE

ingredients

1 recipe	Basic sweet crêpes (recipe follows)
5-6	Sugar cubes
2	Medium sized oranges, washed
100 gms	Butter
3 tbsp	Grand Mariner (orange liqueur)
$2/_3$ cup	Fresh orange juice
½ cup	Castor sugar
3 tbsp	Brandy

method

Make the sweet crêpes as per directions and set aside, covered, to avoid drying. To make orange butter, rub the sugar cubes over the oranges to extract the zest from the rind. Crush the cubes in a bowl with the back of a wooden spoon. With a small sharp knife, peel the oranges. Discard the white pith on the inside of the rind. Chop the rind very finely and add it to the bowl with the mashed sugar cubes. Add half the castor sugar and butter. With the back of a wooden spoon, cream the butter, sugar and rind together until light and fluffy. Work in 4 tbsp orange juice and the Grand Mariner and beat until the mixture is creamy. In a small frying pan, melt the orange butter over a low flame. Holding the outer edges of the crêpe with your fingertips, dip it into the heated butter mixture until well soaked. Carefully fold the crêpe in half, then fold it again into a quarter. Transfer it to a shallow serving dish. Repeat the process with the remaining crêpes until they are all coated. Add the remaining sugar and orange juice to the remaining butter mixture and pour this over the crêpes. When you want to serve take a rounded metal spoon, heat the brandy over a low flame. Do not let it boil. Flambé this over the crêpes. When the flame dies down, serve with vanilla ice cream.

Serves 6-8

Chocolate Fondue

ingredients

6oz or 150gms	Unsweetened chocolate
1 cup	Fresh cream
1½ cups	Powered sugar
½ cup	Butter
3 tbsp	Crème de cacao OR Milk OR Orange
	A small pinch of salt

For Dipping
Sponge cake pieces
Whole strawberries
Apple cubes
Banana slices
Orange sections

method

Place the chocolate pieces in the upper vessel of a double boiler and melt it over hot water. Stir in the sugar, butter and salt. Stir until smooth. Beat the cream separately and add to the chocolate mixture. Stir in the liqueur. Pour into the fondue pot and let it simmer over the burner. Serve with pieces of cake and fruits of your choice with long fondue forks or skewers.

Note You can use Toblerone chocolate instead of unsweetened. But you reduce sugar to ¾ cup.

CHOCOLATE CUPS WITH STRAWBERRY CREAM

ingredients

175 gms	Semisweet cooking chocolate
15 gms	Butter
225 gms	Strawberries, washed and thinly sliced
$\frac{1}{3}$ cup/150 ml	Thick cream
2 tbsp	Icing sugar

method

Break the chocolate into small pieces and heat with butter over hot water until melted and smooth, stirring occasionally to blend well. Take out 8 paper cups for use. Holding each case at an angle, dribble some chocolate into it, a tsp at a time, until the whole cup is thinly coated. Repeat with the remaining cups. Chill for about 30 minutes or until set. (You could do this in two batches to avoid thickening of the chocolate.) Remove one paper case at a time from the refrigerator and peel off the paper, leaving a chocolate cup. Stand the cups on a chilled serving plate until required for further use. To make the filling, whip the cream with icing sugar until stiff peaks form. Gently fold in the strawberries, reserving some for the decoration, and keep cold. Just before serving, fill the cups with the strawberry mixture and decorate with strawberry slices.

variations for the filling

Orange Cream 100 gms fresh cream, 2 tbsp orange liqueur or orange essence, 4-5 slices fresh oranges, peeled, 4 tbsp custard
Cocoa Cream $\frac{1}{3}$ cup cream + 3 tbsp icing sugar, to which you fold in 3 tbsp cocoa powder and ½ tsp vanilla essence

Serves 6-8

KAHLUA CHOCOLATE MOUSSE

ingredients

250 gms	Dark cooking chocolate
125 gms	Butter
4	Eggs
4 tbsp	Powdered sugar
100 gms	Fresh cream
2 tbsp	Kahlua
	A pinch of salt

To Decorate
Whipped cream
Chocolate curls

method

Melt the chocolate in a medium sized bowl over a saucepan filled with simmering water. Separate the eggs: whites in a bigger bowl and yolks in a smaller bowl. Cut the butter into small chunks. When the chocolate has melted, whisk until smooth. Remove the bowl from the heat, add butter and whisk until all the lumps have melted. Add egg yolks. Continue to whisk, until smooth. With dry beaters, whisk egg whites and salt together, adding sugar slowly as the egg white reaches a soft peak stage. Stop when the whites are stiff, but not dry. Scrape the chocolate mixture into a large bowl and fold in the whites. Whip the cream with Kahlua until stiff and fold into the mousse. Pour this into a big bowl or into individual stem glasses and set for 2-4 hours. For best result set it overnight. Decorate with piped cream and chocolate curls.

THE CHEESECAKE

ingredients

For the Base

300 gms	Digestive biscuits
50 gms	Melted butter
¼ cup	Powdered sugar

For the Cheesecake

250 gms	Philadelphia cream cheese
3	Eggs, separated
100 gms	Castor sugar
300 ml	Double cream
4½ tsp	Gelatine mixed with 5 tbsp liquid

method

Liquidise the biscuits in a blender to crumble them, or you could break the biscuits up on greaseproof paper, cover them with another piece and firmly push a rolling pin to and fro until the biscuits become crumbs. Turn the crumbs out into a bowl and fold in the melted butter. Line the base and sides of a loose bottomed cake tin approx. 9-10 inches with the biscuit crumbs and press with the back of your hand to spread evenly. Cook this in an oven at 350°F for 15 minutes and leave it to cool.

Mix the gelatine with water or any other liquid, according to the flavour of the cheesecake you wish to use and soak for 5 minutes. Gently heat on a slow flame. Cook until the liquid is transparent, remove from the stove and cool the mixture, stirring constantly. Set aside. Lightly beat the egg yolks and beat these into the cream cheese with the sugar and then lightly whipped double cream.

Add the relevant flavourings (see individual recipes). Fold in the stiffly beaten egg whites. Now reheat the gelatine over very low heat and melt the mixture. Use a very fine sieve through which you pass the gelatine. Fold straight into the cheese mixture by making gentle sweeping movements. Pour the mixture onto the cooled biscuit base and place it in the fridge to set. When it is set and firm, loosen the sides of the cake from the tin and simply push the base upwards and discard the ring of the tin. Place this on a decorative plate and pipe some fresh cream and pieces of the relevant fruit or flavoring used for the cheesecake. Keep it chilled until ready to serve.

Lemon Cheesecake Fold in the juice and rind of 2 lemons into the basic mixture. You may also add lemon liqueur with the juice.

Kiwi Cheesecake You will need 5 Kiwi fruits. Liquidise 2 of the kiwi fruits with 1 tbsp Kiwi liqueur and 1 tbsp icing sugar. Line cooled base with extra slices of kiwi and fill half the cheese mixture. As it sets, spread further kiwi slices on the top and then cover with remaining cheesecake mixture. Decorate with sweetened cream and kiwi slices or an orchid flower in the centre.

Strawberry Cheesecake You will need 500 gms strawberries. Liquidise ½ of the strawberries with 1 tbsp brandy and 1 tbsp icing sugar. Proceed the same way as the kiwi recipe.

Coffee, Rum and Walnut Cheesecake Add 2 tbsp camp coffee essence and 2 tbsp of any coffee liqueur to the basic recipe and mix gelatine for this recipe with 3 tbsp of rum and 2 tbsps of water. Line the cooled crumb base with 2 tbsp chopped walnuts and pour ½ the cheesecake mixture. When set, put in more walnuts and the rest of the cheesecake mixture. Decorate with piped cream and toasted walnuts.

Serve chilled

Eggless Cheesecake

ingredients

For the Base

300 gms	Digestive biscuit
50 gms	Melted butter
¼ cup	Powdered sugar

For the Cheesecake

200 gms	Philadelphia cream cheese
200 gms	Condensed milk (Milkmaid)
100 gms	Fresh cream
5 gms	China grass mixed with 5 tbsp water OR
4 tsp	Gelatine mixed with 5 tbsp water or liquid

method

Make the crust as per regular cheesecake recipe. Bake and cool. Place the cream cheese and condensed milk in the liquidiser jar. Liquidise both these together and turn in out in a large bowl. Beat the cream till thick and add to the cheese mixture and gently fold in the preferred flavouring as shown in The cheesecake recipe, spoon by spoon. Mix China grass or gelatine with water or preferred liquid and gently heat it when it is transparent. Take it off the stove, cool it by stirring constantly. Strain through a fine sieve and fold into the basic mixture gently. Pour this into a prepared tin. Serve chilled.

Serves 6-8

KIWI BLACK FOREST CAKE

ingredients

1	7" round chocolate sponge cake
300 gms	Fresh cream
6 + 2 tbsp	Powdered sugar
2	Kiwis, peeled and sliced
1 tsp	Lemon juice

To Decorate
Grated chocolate
Whipped cream

method

Cut the sponge cake horizontally through the centre and soak it with sugar water made with 2 tbsp sugar dissolved in water. Beat the cream over a bowl of ice cubes. Gradually add sugar and finally add lemon juice and continue beating till stiff. Spread half the cream over the bottom part of the cake, arrange half of the sliced kiwi on the cream. Cover this with the other half of the cake. Pipe or spread the remaining cream and arrange the remaining kiwi on top. Decorate with chocolate and keep chilled until ready to serve.

Note You could dissolve 2 tbsp sugar in Kiwi liqueur instead of water.

CHOCOLATE FUDGE BROWNIES

ingredients

½ cup	Plain sifted flour
¼ tsp	Baking powder
¼ tsp	Salt
½ cup	Butter (softened)
½ cup	Sugar (powdered)
½ cup	Brown sugar
2	Eggs
250 gms	Unsweetened cooking chocolate (melted)
½ tsp	Vanilla essence
1 cup	Chopped walnuts

To Serve

100 gms	Fresh cream
3 tbsp	Powdered sugar
	A pinch of cinnamon powder

To Sprinkle

1 tbsp	Powdered sugar

method

Pre heat the oven to 325°F. Lightly grease an 8 x 8 x 2 inch baking pan. `Sift flour with baking powder and salt. In a small bowl with an electric mixer, beat the butter with the sugar at high speed till fluffy; beat in eggs, one at a time, until light. Then beat in the melted chocolate and vanilla. At low speed blend in the flour mixture just until combined. Stir in the nuts. Turn into prepared pan and spread evenly. Bake for 30 minutes. Cool for 10 minutes. With a sharp knife, cut into squares. Let it cool completely in the pan, and then remove and arrange them onto a serving plate. Sprinkle with 1 tbsp powdered sugar and serve with fresh cream.

For the Cream

In a chilled stainless steel bowl beat cream at a low speed, add sugar spoon by spoon and cinnamon. When it reaches soft peaks, chill it in the fridge till ready to serve.

Makes 16 pieces

EGGLESS CHOCOLATE FUDGE BROWNIES

ingredients

½ cup	Plain sifted flour
1 tsp	Baking powder
¼ tsp	Salt
¼ cup	Butter (softened)
¼ cup + 1 tbsp	Sugar (powdered)
¼ cup	Brown sugar
½ tin	Condensed milk
250 gms	Unsweetened cooking chocolate (melted)
½ tsp	Vanilla essence
1 cup	Chopped walnuts
2 tbsp	Milk

method

Preheat the oven to 325°F. Lightly grease an 8 x 8 x 2 inch baking pan. Sift flour with baking powder and salt. In a small bowl beat butter with sugar using an electric mixer at high speed, till fluffy. Beat condensed milk, until light. Then beat in the melted chocolate and vanilla. At low speed blend in the flour mixture until just combined. Add milk. Stir in the nuts. Turn into a prepared pan and spread evenly. Bake for 30 minutes. Cool for 10 minutes. With a sharp knife, cut into squares. Let it cool completely in the pan, and then remove and arrange on a serving plate and sprinkle with 1 tbsp of powdered sugar and serve with fresh cream.

SIZZLING BROWNIES

ingredients

8 pieces	Brownies, warmed
1 ½ cups	Hot chocolate sauce (recipe follows)
8 scoops	Vanilla or After 8 ice cream
1 tbsp	Butter to grease the sizzler pan

method

For the Sauce

Heat ¼ cup of milk mixed with ¼ cup of water along with ¼ cup butter until smooth. Add ½ cup of powdered sugar and stir until the sugar dissolves. Add 3-4 tbsp sieved cocoa powder and a pinch of salt. Stir until smooth.

To Serve the Sizzler

Heat the iron sizzler plate directly on the stove, brush it with butter and place the warmed brownie pieces on it. Keep the chocolate sauce boiling hot in a separate vessel. Now place the iron plate on the wooden plate, place a scoop of vanilla ice cream neatly over each brownie and take it to the table. At the table, pour the hot chocolate sauce over it and a little on the sides as well. Let it sizzle and serve immediately.

Serves 6-8

CHOCOLATE WALNUT FUDGE

ingredients

450 gms	Castor sugar
150 ml(¼ pint)	Milk
100 gms	Plain cooking chocolate
50 gms	Maple syrup or honey
150 gms	Butter
100 gms	Chopped walnuts
	A pinch of salt

method

Grease an 8" x 6" tin. Mix together sugar, salt, milk, chocolate and honey/maple syrup in a large thick saucepan over gentle heat. Stir constantly until the sugar has dissolved. Bring to a boil until it reaches the soft ball stage. Remove from heat, add the butter and leave it to cool for about 5 minutes without stirring. Then, beat the mixture until thick and creamy. Add the chopped nuts all at once and stir with a wooden spoon until they are mixed into the fudge. Immediately pour this into the greased tin. Leave it until it is completely cold. Then cut the fudge into squares and remove from the tin and serve.

Fresh Strawberry Glaze Pie

ingredients

9 inch	Baked pie shell

For the Glaze

2½ cups	Medium or small strawberries, washed
1 cup	Castor or powdered sugar
2½ tbsp	Corn flour
1 tbsp	Butter

For the Filling

4 cups	Large strawberries, halved
2 tbsp	Cointreau or orange juice

To Serve
Vanilla ice cream or sweetened cream

method

Make the glaze; crush the strawberries and combine with sugar and corn flour along with ½ cup water and bring to a boil until the mixture thickens and is translucent. Strain, add butter and cool. Gently toss the large strawberries with the Cointreau or orange juice. Let it stand for 30 minutes. Then, arrange them in the pie shell. Pour the cool glaze over the strawberries. Refrigerate until chilled, for about 2 hours. Garnish with cream or serve with ice cream.

Serves 8-10

FLAMBÉD STRAWBERRIES WITH VANILLA ICE CREAM

ingredients

1 kg	Vanilla ice cream
500 gms	Medium sized strawberries, washed with the stems removed
2 tsp	Lemon juice
5-6 tbsp	Powdered sugar
4 tbsp	Orange juice (optional)
2 tsp	Butter
¼ cup	Brandy
2 tsp	Strawberry liqueur (optional)

method

Soak the strawberries in orange juice, lemon juice, strawberry liqueur and sugar for about ½ an hour. When you want to serve, place a small burner on the table. Heat a frying pan, melt the butter and put the strawberries soaked in juice into it. Let them cook until semi soft. Pour the brandy into a ladle and heat over the burner and slightly tilt the spoon so that the brandy catches the flame and pour this over the strawberries. Serve right away with vanilla ice cream.

HONEY-NUT ICE CREAM

ingredients

1½ litres	Milk
2 tbsp	Corn flour
1½ cups	Sugar
1 tsp	Gelatine, dissolved in 3 tbsp water
200 gms	Fresh cream
¼ cup each	Finely chopped walnuts and cashews
½ cup	Chopped dried figs
¼ cup	Honey
¼ cup	Water

method

Boil the milk for 30 minutes. Dissolve corn flour in a little cold milk and add to the boiling milk along with sugar. Stir constantly until thick. Remove from the stove and cool. Add the melted gelatine and fresh cream. Combine the walnuts, cashews, figs, honey and water in a small saucepan and heat on the stove. Then cool. Add to the prepared milk. Cover the pan and chill for 15-20 minutes. Then make ice cream in a churner. Transfer it to a metal box and freeze it.

DARSAAN
Honey Coated Fried Noodles

ingredients

For the Noodles

1 cup	Plain flour
3 tsp	Oil
½ tsp	Salt
	A pinch of baking powder
	Oil for frying

For the Sauce

2 tbsp	Sugar
2 tbsp	Honey

To Garnish
Almond flakes

To Serve
Vanilla or Butterscotch ice cream

method

Sieve the flour with baking powder and salt. Make a well in the centre and pour the oil in. Mix with your fingertips and make a soft dough by adding cold water. Cover and set aside for ½ an hour. Roll out a 9 inch round and roll it like a Swiss roll. Cut it though 1 cm. wide and open up the strips. Fry them in hot oil. While the noodles are frying, make the sauce as follows.

In a small saucepan mix together sugar with 2 tbsp water and heat on a slow flame. When the sugar melts add the honey and mix well. Take it off the stove. Remove the fried noodles onto a serving dish and pour the honey sauce over it. Garnish with almond flakes and serve immediately with vanilla or butterscotch ice cream.

PERFECT APPLE PIE

ingredients

For the Pastry

2 cups	Plain flour, sifted
1 cup	Butter (cold)
4 tbsp	Light brown sugar
2-4 tbsp	Cold water

For the Filling

7 cups	Thinly sliced cooking apples
1 cup	Sugar
1 tsp	Powdered cinnamon
3 tbsp	Raisins, stemmed and washed
2 tbsp	Plain flour
2 tbsp	Lemon juice
2 tbsp	Butter
	A pinch of salt

method

For the Pastry

In a medium sized mixing bowl, combine the flour and sugar. Cut the butter into small cubes and rub this into the flour with your fingertips until it resembles breadcrumbs. Add 2 tbsp cold water and mix well to make a smooth dough. Add more water if the dough is too dry. Form the dough into a ball, wrap it in a towel and chill for 30 minutes before using.

Divide the dough into 2 halves. Roll out half in a 12" circle with a rolling pin. Roll from the centre outwards. Place a 9" pie dish on the pastry circle; the pastry should be 1" wider all around. Carefully transfer the pastry to the pie dish. Press it gently with your fingers to fix it around snugly. Refrigerate for 15 minutes. Prick it all around with a fork and bake in the oven at 200°C or 400°F for 10-15 minutes.

For the Filling

In a small bowl mix the sugar, flour, cinnamon and salt. In another bowl, toss apples with lemon juice. Add sugar mixture to the apples and toss lightly to combine. Turn into the pastry lined pie dish, mounding up in the centre to support the top crust. Roll out the remaining dough into a 12" circle. Fold it over in quarters; cut slits for steam vents. Place the pastry in the centre and unfold to seal neatly. Crimp the edges. Bake for 45 minutes until apples are tender and the crust golden. Let it cool for 5-7 minutes before you serve.

PEACH AND PLUM FLAN

ingredients

For the Filling

2	Fresh peaches
4	Fresh plums
1	Lemon
6 tbsp	Sugar

For the Glaze

4 tbsp	Red jelly
2 tbsp	Water

For the Flan Case

4 tbsp	Butter
3 tbsp	Honey
2 tbsp	Brown sugar
175 gms	Muesli (half crushed in a food processor)

To Serve
Fresh cream or vanilla ice cream

method

To make the flan case, melt 3 tbsp of the butter, honey and sugar in a saucepan over low heat. Boil gently for 30 seconds. Remove from heat and stir in the cereal. Grease a 7" flan ring or pie tin with 1 tbsp of butter and line it with the mixture. Press the mixture well to the base and sides. Bake in the centre of a moderate oven for 8-10 minutes till it is golden brown. Remove it from the oven and let it cool. When the mixture is firm, gradually ease it onto the serving plate.

To make the filling, remove the skin from both the fruits and slice them vertically into 6 pieces each. You will need two small saucepans, one for each fruit. Mix 3 tbsp sugar with the peach slices and cook them on a slow flame until soft, yet firm in consistency. Repeat the same with the plums.

Arrange peaches along the rim of the flan and the plums at the centre. Make the glaze by heating the jelly and water together. Cool it slightly and brush it over the fruit. Chill it in the fridge until you are ready to serve. This dish can also be served at room temperature, with sweetened whipped cream or ice cream.

BAKLAVA

Baklava is a light, crisp, and delicate Middle Eastern pastry. Layers of phylo-pastry sandwiched with a pistachio and walnut mixture and poured over with sugar syrup makes it a sinful, all time favourite dish.

ingredients

For the Pastry

500 gms	Phylo or puff pastry dough
100 gms	Shortening or unsalted butter
300 gms	Pistachio, walnuts or almonds, finely ground

For the Syrup

250 gms	Sugar
150 ml	Water
2 tbsp	Lemon juice
1 tsp	Powdered saffron

To Sprinkle

50 gms	Coarsely ground nuts

method

Buy phylo or puff pastry readymade from any bakery. You will need a Swiss roll tin approx. 10"x 11". Preheat the oven to 325ºF. Grease the dish with butter or shortening. Roll out the dough very lightly using a little flour if required to match the size of the tin. Place this on the greased tin and brush it with butter. Spread the nuts of your choice over the pastry. Cover with the remaining pastry brushing with butter. You could make several layers of this if you wish, brushing each one with shortening or butter. Finally seal the pastry from the sides and cut diagonally with a sharp knife. Bake the Baklava for 45 minutes in a preheated oven (325°F) then raise the heat to 425°F and bake for 15 minutes more.

The Baklava should be golden in colour.
While it is baking, prepare the syrup thick enough to coat a spoon.
Allow it to cool completely. Add lemon juice and saffron. Remove
Baklava from the oven and quickly pour the cold syrup over the
hot Baklava. Cut into pieces and place them on a serving dish,
sprinkled with coarsely ground almonds or pistachio mixed with
a little sugar syrup. Serve hot or cold.

Makes 35 pieces

CHOCOLATE WAFFLES

ingredients

½ cup	Butter
1½ cups	Plain flour
1 cup	Sugar
1 tsp	Baking powder
¼ tsp	Salt
2 squares	Chocolate, melted over hot water
½ cup	Milk
2	Eggs, separated
½ tsp	Vanilla

To Serve
Hot maple syrup or whipped cream or ice cream

method

Cream the butter and sugar. Add well-beaten egg yolks and
melted chocolate. Mix thoroughly. Sift the measured flour with
baking powder and salt. Add this dry mixture alternately with
milk to the chocolate mixture. Add vanilla and fold in stiffly
beaten egg whites. Bake in a hot waffle iron for 8-10 minutes
serve with hot maple syrup, cream or ice cream.

Makes 4 waffles

DATE AND ALMOND SQUARES

ingredients

For the Date Mixture

450 gms	Dates, chopped coarsely
8 tbsp	Brown sugar, powdered
1 tbsp	Flour
1 cup	Water
1 tsp	Vanilla essence

For the Pastry

1 cup	Plain flour
1 tsp	Soda } Sieved together
	A pinch of salt
1 cup	Powdered brown sugar
1 cup	Butter, melted
1 cup	Powdered almonds
	Butter for greasing 9" x 12" tray

method

To prepare the date mixture, mix together dates, sugar, flour and water in a pan. Cook until thick, stirring occasionally. Take it off the stove, add vanilla, mix well and set aside. To make the pastry, add the almonds and sugar to the sieved flour mixture and mix well. Add cooled melted butter and mix well to form a soft dough. Divide the pastry in half and spread over the prepared baking tray. Top it up with the date mixture and cover the rest of the pastry. Bake in a preheated oven at 180°C for 30 minutes. Leave to cool. When cool, cut into even squares and serve.

Makes 24 pieces

ORANGE-CHOCOLATE MOUSSE

ingredients

5 gms	China grass or 4 tsp Gelatine
6 tbsp	Orange juice
½ cup	Sugar
¼ cup	Cocoa powder + A pinch of salt
¼ cup	Water
2 tbsp	Milk
1 tsp	Orange essence
¼ tsp	Freshly grated orange peel
200 gms	Cream

method

Soak China grass or gelatine in orange juice and let it stand for 1 minute. Cook over a slow flame till the China grass dissolves and becomes a transparent liquid. Take it off the heat and cool it by stirring continuously. In a small saucepan, combine sugar, cocoa and water. Cook over low heat, stirring constantly, until slightly thickened. Remove from heat, add China grass or gelatine mixture and stir until dissolved. Blend in the milk, vanilla and cool it. In a small mixer bowl, combine whipped cream and orange peel. Beat until stiff. Gradually add chocolate mixture to the whipped cream. Spoon into dessert dishes and refrigerate for 1 hour.
Serve chilled.

Butterscotch Praline Sundae

ingredients

For the Sundae

½ kg	Vanilla ice cream
½ kg	Butterscotch ice cream
1 cup	Praline sauce

For the Praline Sauce

¼ cup	Butter
½ cup	Brown sugar
2 tbsp	Maple syrup
¼ cup	Water
1 tsp	Rum or Brandy
½ cup	Finely chopped nuts (almonds, walnuts, cashews, or a mixture of all three)

method

Semi soften the ice cream in separate bowls and press it down in the desired tin forming 2 layers (vanilla and butterscotch). Freeze it overnight.

To make the sauce, heat the butter over medium heat until golden, and cool. Gradually add sugar, mixing until smooth. Stir in the syrup and water. Bring to a boil and stir for 1 minute. Cool slightly, then stir in the rum/brandy and nuts. When you want to serve, unmould the ice cream onto a serving plate, pour the warm sauce over it and serve.

Serves 4-6

PEACH AND APPLE COBBLER

ingredients

For the Filling

1 kg	Ripe peaches
1	Large apples
½ cup	Sugar
½ cup	Cinnamon
2 tbsp	Plain flour
1 tbsp	Lemon juice

For the Topping

1 cup	Plain flour
1 tsp	Baking powder
¼ tsp	Salt
½ tsp	Vanilla
4 tbsp	Butter
3 tbsp	Cream
	A pinch of soda
1 egg OR	
3 tbsp	Condensed milk

method

Peel and slice the peaches and apples, add the sugar and lemon juice. Mix the flour and cinnamon together and toss with the fruit. Set this mixture aside in a saucepan. Preheat the oven (400°F).

To make the topping, combine all the dry ingredients. Cut the butter into small cubes and rub into the flour until they resemble breadcrumbs. Mix the cream, vanilla and egg or condensed milk together, and add this mixture to the dry ingredients. Mix everything together. With the help of a little flour on your palms, make circles 2½" diameter and about ½" thickness. Set aside.

Take an 8-cup-capacity baking dish. Heat the apple and peach mixture until the juices begin to boil. Pour this mixture into a baking dish and lay the rounds over the surface. Sprinkle a little sugar on top and bake until the top is brown. Remove from the oven and let it rest for 5 minutes. Serve immediately with vanilla ice cream.

BACI
Chocolate-Walnut Kisses

ingredients

200 gms	Walnuts, roasted and finely chopped
200 gms	Thick cream
250 gms	Dark cooking chocolate
3-4 tbsp	Icing sugar
2 tbsp	Dark rum
	A pinch of salt
32	Small paper cups

method

Heat the cream in a pan and melt the chocolate, stirring constantly. Once melted and incorporated with the cream, remove from heat and add sugar, salt and rum. Cool until just firm. Set 3-4 tiny pieces of walnuts in each paper cup. Beat the chocolate mixture until smooth and fill the chocolate mixture in a piping bag with a star nozzle. Pipe a whirl of chocolate over the nuts in each cup and cool until firm. They will stay in the fridge for upto one week in an airtight container.

Makes 32 small cups

MOHLET SAUNG
Iced Coconut Milk with Sago

ingredients

1 cup	Sago
4 cups	Water
4 cups	Medium thick coconut milk
½ cup	Water chestnuts (optional)
	A Dash of rose syrup
	Ice cubes
	Rock sugar (white or brown) to taste

method

Wash and soak the sago for approximately 1 hour. Drain and put the sago in a large saucepan with 3 cups of water. Bring to a boil and simmer over moderate heat until the sago grains are clear. Cool and chill. Put the sugar into a small pan with the remaining water and heat gently until the sugar has dissolved. Cool and strain the syrup. Add a dash of rose syrup for colour. Put about 4 tbsp of sago and 2 pieces of water chestnuts (if using) into a stemmed glass, add 3 tbsp of syrup and mix well. Add 2-3 ice cubes and fill up with coconut milk and stir. Serve immediately.

Serves 6-8

GLOSSARY
Of Selected Ingredients and Cooking Terms

A la	In the manner of
Al dente	Cooked until it offers just slight resistance to bite
Appetizer	A first course of a meal of tidbits, drinks or cocktails
Barbecue	To cook on a rack over a charcoal fire or gas
Basil	Fresh or dried, broken or ground leaves with pungent flavour and sweet aroma
Bay leaf	Whole dry leaf or ground, with strong flavour especially if whole leaf torn or crushed
Bean-curd	Tofu or soybean cake
Boucheé	Small puff pastry patty, with savoury filling
Canapé	An appetizer consisting of a firm base of bread, toast, pastry etc with savoury and decorative topping
Castor sugar	Refined white sugar
Chives	Member of onion family. Long spiky green leaves
Chowder	A thick American style soup
Cinnamon	Reddish brown stick of rolled bark with sweet pungent aroma
Condensed milk	Evaporated milk to which sugar has been added
Coriander	Whole seeds or fresh leaves with slightly orange flavour and aroma
Crépe	A thin flour-based pancake used to fill savoury or sweet mixtures
Crudité	A variety of fresh raw vegetables cut long and served ice cold with a dip or by itself
Croquettes	A soft mixture of vegetables and seasoning, rolled into oval shapes coated with bread crumbs or vermicelli and fried
Croûtons	Small pieces of bread, fried or toasted
Cumin	Whole seeds or ground with strong and slightly bitter flavour
Curry powder	A blend of many spices giving a distinctive flavour
Falafel	Dumplings made from different pulses or vegetables
Fondue	A dish cooked on the table usually over a spirit heater. A Swiss fondue is of melted cheese and wine served with chunks of bread
Fritter	A portion of batter coated food, deep-fried until crisp
Galangal	Thai variety of ginger
Gelatine	Unflavoured jelly crystal used to set the mixture
Ginger	Whole roots fresh or dried, pungent or hot

Jalapeño peppers	Spicy Mexican chillies of green variety
Kaffir lime leaves	Leaves of Thai lime tree, used for flavouring in Thai food
Marinate	A seasoned liquid usually a blend of oil, wine, vinegar and seasonings to coat food and add flavour
Marjoram	Fresh or dried leaves with spicy, slightly bitter flavour
Meringue	A crisp egg white and sugar mixture whisked and baked
Mint	Fresh or dried leaves with strong, sweet aroma and cool after taste
Miso	Fermented soy bean paste
Monterey Jack cheese	Tangy Mexican cheese
Mozzarella cheese	Special tangy Italian cheese widely used for pizzas etc
MSG	Monosodium Glutamate, a seasoning often used to flavour Chinese food.
Nutmeg	Large whole seeds or ground with warm sweet aromatic flavour
Oregano	Dried or fresh leaves with strong flavour
Palm sugar	Unrefined brown sugar
Parboil	To boil for part of the normal cooking time
Parsley	Fresh leaves and stems with very strong flavour
Pâté	A minced or finely chopped savoury puree sealed in a mould and served as dip
Peppercorn	Red coloured peppercorn
Pine nuts	One of the popular nuts widely used in Middle-Eastern cooking
Pita bread	Lebanese, flat bread either made with plain flour or whole wheat
Praline	Sugar flavoured with coarsely ground roasted nut
Quiche	An open custard tart with savory or sweet filling
Raw sugar	Unrefined white sugar
Roulade	Soufflé type mixture baked and served in a roll with various filling
Roux	A thick sauce made with flour, butter and milk
Sake	Rice wine
Seasoning	Salt, pepper, spices, herbs etc., added to give depth of flavour
Sichuan Togarashi	Japanese chilli powder
Simmer	To cook in a liquid at a temperature just below boiling point

Stir fry	To cook quickly in a little oil stirring constantly
Stock	The liquid produced when vegetables are simmered in water for a long period to extract the flavour
Sun-dried tomatoes	Tomatoes that are dried in the sun for a number of days and then stored or preserved in olive oil
Taco seasoning mix	A special blend of Mexican spice that is combination of dried onion, garlic, chillies and other spices
Tahina	Sesame purée
Tamarind	Fruit of tamarind tree with sharp sour taste
Tarragon	Fresh or dried with sweet, aromatic and piquant flavour
Thyme	Fresh or dried or ground with pungent aromatic flavour
To bake	To cook in the oven by dry heat
To beat	A thin liquid mixed with an eggbeater to incorporate air and to thicken it gradually. This method is also used to make a mixture smooth and free from lumps
To blanch	To treat food with boiling water, loosen the skin and remove
To chill	To cool food without freezing in the refrigerator
To fry	To cook in hot oil
To flambé	To ignite alcohol and pour the burning liquor on the finished dish
To fold in	To combine a light whisked mixture with other ingredients so that it retains its lightness
To grease	To coat the surface of a dish with fat to prevent sticking
To purée	To press food through a fine sieve in a blender or a food processor, to a smooth, thick mixture
To sauté	To cook in an open pan in hot, shallow fat, tossing the food to prevent sticking
To sieve	To rub or press moist or dry food through a sieve
To shred	To slice food into very thin pieces
To steam	To cook in the steam of boiling water without food touching water
To toss	Two or more ingredients are mixed together without mashing with a fork
Tortilla	Thin, Mexican flat bread made with maize flour or plain flour
Tostada	Tortilla fried until crisp and served flat topped with beans or savoury mixture
Vinegar	Generally made from malt, cider, sugarcane, or grape juice to add sour taste to many dishes
Wok	A Chinese cooking pan
Zatar spice mix	Lebanese spice that is a combination of thyme, sesame, salt etc.